# CONTENTS

## CREDITS

**Produced by the Games Workshop Design Studio**

© Copyright Games Workshop Limited 2013, Games Workshop, the Games Workshop logo, GW, Warhammer, Warhammer 40,000, the Warhammer 40,000 logo, the Aquila logo, 40K, 40,000, Citadel, the Citadel Device, Clan Raukaan - A Codex: Space Marines, Supplement and all associated marks, logos, names, places, characters, creatures, races and race insignia, illustrations and images from the Warhammer 40,000 universe are either ®, TM and/ or © Games Workshop Ltd 2000-2013 variably registered in the UK and other countries around the world. All Rights Reserved.

British Cataloguing-in-Publication Data. A catalogue record for this book is available from the British Library. Pictures used for illustrative purposes only.

Certain Citadel products may be dangerous if used incorrectly and Games Workshop does not recommend them for use by children under the age of 16 without adult supervision. Whatever your age, be careful when using glues, bladed equipment and sprays and make sure that you read and follow the instructions on the packaging.

| **UK** | **NORTHERN EUROPE** | **NORTH AMERICA** | **AUSTRALIA** |
|---|---|---|---|
| Games Workshop Ltd, Willow Rd, Lenton, Nottingham, NG7 2WS | Games Workshop Ltd, Willow Rd, Lenton, Nottingham, NG7 2WS | Games Workshop Inc, 6211 East Holmes Road, Memphis, Tennessee 38141 | Games Workshop, 23 Liverpool Street, Ingleburn, NSW 2565 |

# INTRODUCTION

**Clan Raukaan, the Iron Hands 3rd Company, are masters of the sledgehammer armoured offensive. Implacable, conquering warriors, the battle-brothers of Clan Company Raukaan have a caged fury in their hearts that few foes can stand against.**

The Iron Hands are amongst the oldest and proudest of the Space Marine Chapters. They suffered more than most during the Horus Heresy, and the deep-rooted scars left on their Chapter's soul have left them deeply embittered. The Chapter fights on in defence of the Emperor's realm, utilising blunt, merciless strategies and logistical superiority to crush their enemies utterly. The Iron Hands hold to the creed of iron over flesh, bionically augmenting their battle-brothers to an ever-greater extent in the belief that the weaknesses of the flesh must be excised at all costs. The Chapter's every action is calculated to avoid the slightest display of weakness, for above all they fear to repeat the failings of their lost Primarch and believe that only through cold logic and relentless strength can they avoid this fate.

Within the ranks of the Iron Hands, Clan Company Raukaan are notorious for allowing their emotions to govern their actions more than any of their brothers. Though many of the Chapter's Iron Fathers believe this trait to be the Clan Company's inherent weakness, it is in fact their greatest strength; indeed, the caged fires in the hearts of Clan Company Raukaan may yet prove the salvation of everything that their Chapter holds dear...

## HOW TO USE THIS BOOK

If you are reading this codex supplement, then you have already taken your first steps into the Warhammer 40,000 hobby. The *Warhammer 40,000* rulebook contains all the rules you need to fight battles with your Citadel miniatures, while *Codex: Space Marines* contains everything you need to field a force of Space Marines in these games.

This codex supplement allows you to turn your collection of Space Marines into an unstoppable army of merciless Iron Hands from the 3rd Company, Clan Raukaan. It tells the dramatic story of Clan Company Raukaan's wars, spanning the last ten thousand years; it details their victories, their defeats, and the constant battle they have fought against the terrible flaw lurking deep within the psyche of their Chapter. You'll also find a showcase of beautifully painted Space Marines miniatures showing the colour scheme and iconography of Clan Company Raukaan. Finally, this book includes new missions, both to recreate the famous battles fought by Clan Company Raukaan, and to reflect their favoured tactics, as well as unique relics, Warlord Traits, and new stratagems to bring to bear in your games of Planetstrike and Cities of Death.

# THE CLAN COMPANIES

**The Iron Hands Chapter comprises ten clan companies, each a brotherhood one hundred warriors strong, and a formidable army in its own right. Each possesses its own unique qualities, and each has a different role within the Chapter.**

Though the cause of every Chapter of Adeptus Astartes is the same, their means and methods often differ. This is especially true of those Chapters originating from the First Founding. Descended from the warriors who followed their Primarchs to war, these Chapters' identities are strongly influenced by the Legions they once were, and by the scars they still bear from the dark days of the Horus Heresy. The truth of this is seen clearly in the cold and embittered brethren of the Iron Hands.

A Chapter who despise the weakness of flesh above all, the Iron Hands bear a scar upon their collective soul that drives them to seek the purity and perfection of the machine. On the killing fields of Isstvan V their Primarch, Ferrus Manus, was the first of his brotherhood of demigods to fall. He was cut down by Fulgrim, the traitorous master of the Emperor's Children, and there are many among the Iron Hands who believe that it was an excess of furious choler that led their Primarch to his doom. Thus the Iron Hands as a Chapter are driven to embrace logic and mechanical precision lest they fall prey to the same error that claimed their gene-father. They bury their bile beneath strings of dispassionate numbers, and purge their flesh in favour of the cold certainty of the machine.

## ANACHRONISTIC TRAITS

Despite all this, the Iron Hands are a brotherhood riddled with strange contradictions. While they strive constantly to free themselves from the weakness of emotion, they still hold fiercely to certain traditions which logic alone cannot account for. Amongst the most prominent of these are their clan companies, of which Raukaan is but one. As with all Chapters who adhere to the Codex Astartes, the Iron Hands are organised into ten companies, each composed according to the statutes laid down by Guilliman in his seminal work. Yet where other Chapters simply number these companies one to ten, the clan companies of the Iron Hands instead bear the honorific titles of the ten great clans of Medusa.

These clans were believed – rightly or wrongly – to be the primogenitors of human civilisation on their world, and possessed a near-mythical significance even before the vast upheavals of Ferrus Manus' arrival. Though Medusa possessed a bewildering plethora of minor and major clans, the ten great clans were considered the original and most mighty – the men and women from whom all others of Medusan birth could trace their heritage. To this day, the glowering countenances of the ten clan lords are still carved into the storm-wracked Felgarrthi mountains near the Medusan equator, protected from tectonics and atmospherics by vast stasis generators built during the Dark Age of Technology. Indeed, it is beneath the pitiless gaze of these monolithic statues that the Iron Hands test their potential recruits during the yearly eclipse known as the Iron Moon.

In the aftermath of the Horus Heresy, the guidance of their lost Primarch had been replaced by the collective minds of the Iron Council, and the battered Legion faced division into Chapters. In the days of the Primarch, Manus had always insisted his companies be named after the Medusan clans, believing that bearing these names would remind his sons of their link to the mortal men they had once been, and hold at bay their more aloof, detached tendencies. While the message behind this decision might have been lost with the Primarch's death, it was felt by the Iron Council that certain traditions should be retained, lest the successor Chapters of the Iron Hands be weakened by a loss of identity. The honorific designations of clan companies were one such tradition.

To this day the institution of the clans holds true. Though the battlefield roles of the companies remain as defined by the Codex Astartes – veterans forming the 1st Company and Assault Marines the 8th, for example – their identities are bound into their adopted clan name. Any warrior joining a new company will discard his previous clan allegiances, being considered a member of his newly adoptive clan from that day onward until his death or promotion to a new company. Traditionally, each clan company maintains certain traits and characteristics unique to itself and its ancestors, though this is true of some more than others. For example, the Assault Marines of Clan Borrgar – notorious even on Medusa for its ruthlessness – are noted for their single-minded elimination of their targets, down to the last man.

### CLAN COMPANY AVERNII (1ST COMPANY)

*When Ferrus Manus fell, he was surrounded by his Avernii elite, most of whom were also slain in the maelstrom of carnage that claimed their Primarch. To many among the Iron Hands, the failure of the Avernii to either dissuade their gene-father from his rash course or exhibit the strength and fortitude to keep him alive was an unforgivable frailty. Ten thousand years on, this shadow still hangs over the elite of the Iron Hands. Promotion to veteran status is thus a bittersweet honour within the Chapter, for it also imposes an onerous duty upon the recipient to do better than his ancestors did. No weakness is tolerated within the ranks of Clan Company Avernii, and significant levels of cybernetic augmentation are common.*

# THE AGE OF BETRAYALS

**There is a bitterness within the battle-brothers of the Iron Hands, a resentment that corrodes them daily from within. This hidden vitriol stems from one of the most callous betrayals of the Horus Heresy, and has eaten at the Chapter ever since.**

The Emperor's Great Crusade was the most incredible undertaking in human history. This mighty war of conquest was intended to reunite the human race, dispelling the shadows of Old Night with the light of the Imperial Truth. At the forefront of this war marched the Emperor's mighty sons, the Primarchs, and their Space Marine Legions. Each Legion had its own unique character and way of war, and the Iron Hands were to develop a reputation among their brothers as remarkably single-minded, deadly soldiers.

When Ferrus Manus was discovered on Medusa and reunited with his Legion, he took the bellicose, wrathful warriors he was given to command and reshaped them according to his will. Once bombastic and aggressive, the Iron Hands were bound by their Primarch in fetters of logic and fashioned into a single-minded engine of war that forgave no frailty, whether within or without. They were warriors of conquest, not of deliverance, and they fought at the vanguard of many of the nascent Imperium's greatest and most grindingly bloody campaigns.

However, though the Iron Hands and their brother Legions carried the Imperial Truth to the furthest corners of the galaxy, their dream was fated to fall into shadow. Warmaster Horus – most favoured of the Emperor's sons – fell to the whispered temptations of the Dark Gods. His own insecurity and paranoia was turned against him, the vast burden placed upon his shoulders by the Emperor used to crush his spirit and fashion him into a creature of the Ruinous Powers.

Horus successfully turned many of his brothers to rebellion alongside him. A series of vile betrayals were enacted as these newly Traitor Legions turned upon their old allies with a ferocity reserved for brothers whose love has turned to hate. Amongst the earliest and worst betrayals of the entire Heresy was the horrific battle on Isstvan V; known as the Dropsite Massacre, it was a conflict that would see the Iron Hands' destiny forever changed.

## FALL OF A DEMIGOD

The Iron Hands' Primarch – great Ferrus Manus himself – was the first of the Emperor's sons to fall during the conflict, slain on Isstvan V at the hands of his duplicitous brother Fulgrim. His death would leave a terrible scar upon the soul of the Legion he left behind. The Iron Hands themselves were to sustain brutal casualties during the Dropsite Massacre and in its aftermath, elements of Manus' forces rushing blindly into traitor ambushes and facing destruction in turn.

Though the Horus Heresy raged for years, the Iron Hands were to play a comparatively minor part in it. With their strength shattered and much of the surviving Legion scattered to the stars, they were forced to establish a new council upon Medusa to rule in the Primarch's stead. Yet though this council fought hard to restore their Legion's strength and strike back at the traitors for the wounds they had suffered, many Iron Hands took months or even years to obey the council's dictates while others – it is claimed – rebelled and deserted their Legion altogether.

By the end of the Heresy, the Iron Hands had won a number of peripheral victories over the traitor forces, but had fallen well short of the crushing catharsis they so desired. This would be just another bitter blow to the Legion's collective soul, a black mark to haunt them in the years to come.

> 'You are all my sons, and the fires of the forge burn as hot in your hearts as they do in mine. Chain them, master them, and you shall wield a deadly weapon. But allow them to rule you, and you shall be lost.'
> *- Ferrus Manus, address to the Legion before the Garvian Crusade*

## AN ANCIENT ORDER

*One of the many anachronisms exhibited by the Iron Hands is their continued use of the rank of Iron Father. The first individuals to bear this title were not of the Legion at all, but were instead engineer-mystics who maintained the Dark Age machineries of the Medusan clans. These original Iron Fathers wielded considerable influence thanks to their vital contribution to life on Medusa, and enjoyed positions in the hierarchy of each clan. When Ferrus Manus forcibly introduced his Legion to the world they would call home, the rank of Iron Father was adapted by those battle-brothers whose duty was the care of the Iron Hands' weapons, vehicles and armaments. Though the title has remained constant over the millennia, its meaning continued to change after the Iron*

*Council's formation – by the dawning of M41 it had come to be an honorific, an additional title awarded to the esteemed individuals who were voted into the ranks of the Iron Council. Any battle-brother of rank within the Iron Hands can become an Iron Father, from mighty Iron Captains, Iron Chaplains and Librarians, to Apothecaries and Veteran Sergeants. Historically, though, the most common recipients of this honour have been the Techmarines and Masters of the Forge – the Iron Hands warriors whose own duties echo those of the Iron Fathers of old. Every clan company must always have at least one Iron Father amongst its ranks – and most will have more – and the word of these individuals will often be heeded by their battle-brothers even over that of higher ranking officers who are not themselves members of the Iron Council.*

## C.M30 THE AGE OF FERRUS

### The Hammer and the Storm
The Iron Hands Legion, named in some records of this time as the Stormwalkers, are committed en masse to the extermination of the Orks of the Krooked Klaw. The Legion that will one day become the Iron Hands prove their merciless dedication to decisive and direct action by utilising a strategy known as the hammer and the storm. Luckless Imperial Army regiments are used as a lure, drawing the majority of the Orks into a single almighty engagement. Once their foes are fully committed the Iron Hands strike with everything they have, their assault turning the battlefield into a meatgrinder that lasts for days on end.

### Rise of the Gorgon
Ferrus Manus, the Primarch of the Iron Hands, is discovered amid the post-industrial ruins of Medusa. Named the Gorgon after a terrifying beast of local folklore, he establishes himself as the cold and unforgiving god-king of the Medusan clans. Soon enough, he does the same with his Legion, forcibly integrating them with the peoples of his adoptive home world and reforging the Iron Hands in his own image.

### Strength through Iron
The Iron Hands Legion win themselves a reputation as cold, merciless conquerors. They are a blunt instrument of lethal intent to be wielded by the commanders of the crusading forces, and are pivotal in a number of major engagements during the Great Crusade. During this time, Ferrus Manus' doctrines of extreme efficiency and strength above all come to the fore, and the first instances are recorded of Iron Hands battle-brothers undergoing voluntary cybernetic augmentation to improve and strengthen the machines that are their bodies. It is said that the Primarch finds this practise disquieting, but permits it to continue nonetheless.

### The Fall of Gardinaal
Ultramarines forces are mired in a brutal war of attrition in the Gardinaal System. The Legions of Ferrus Manus and Fulgrim, by now sworn brothers and close allies, arrive to assist Guilliman's sons. The war that follows is apocalyptic in its brutality, and the warlords of Gardinaal are crushed without mercy.

### Heresy Declared
Horus reveals his treachery and plunges the nascent Imperium into a civil war more bloody and vast in scale than anything Humanity has faced since the darkness of Old Night. At the outset of hostilities, the bulk of the Iron Hands Legion comprises the 52nd Expeditionary Fleet, though many smaller fragments of the Legion's strength are engaged with other Imperial assets elsewhere across the galaxy.

## C.M31 THE AGE OF SORROW

### Overcome by Wrath
When news of the rebellion reaches Ferrus Manus, he is overwhelmed by a fury that is frightening to behold, even for his own warriors. The Primarch's wellspring of wrath bubbles to the surface, overriding the fetters of cold logic and self-restraint that have served him well for so long. In his rage, he races ahead of his Legion to Isstvan V, accompanied only by his chosen elites from Clan Avernii. He arrives in time to join a mighty force of supposedly loyal Adeptus Astartes as they launch their attack against Horus and his traitors.

### Isstvan V Dropsite Massacre
After the Iron Warriors, Night Lords and Word Bearers reveal themselves to be traitors in league with Horus, the loyalist Space Marine forces are outnumbered, surrounded and brutally massacred. Ferrus Manus, forging ahead into battle despite the odds and against the urgings of the other loyalist Legions, is slain in battle with Fulgrim of the Emperor's Children. Manus' Avernii elite are all but wiped out during the battle, and great swathes of the pursuing Iron Hands forces are subsequently annihilated as they rush headlong into ambushes above the planet.

### A Broken Legion
The fractured Iron Hands Legion, reduced to a shadow of its former strength, reels from the monstrous blow dealt to them. Terrible scars are left upon the Legion's collective soul, and many among their number remain in denial about the death of their Primarch.

### The Iron Council
A gathering of clans and Iron Fathers on Medusa forms a new council to rule the Iron Hands now that the Primarch is 'lost'. It is decided that no single individual will ever rule over the Iron Hands again. The newly formed Iron Council concentrate their efforts on replenishing the strength of their shattered Legion, and though the Iron Hands score numerous peripheral victories during the Heresy, they are far from the truly pivotal battles. Dark tales proliferate from this time of Iron Hands factions rebelling altogether or turning to forbidden secrets of techno-heresy that are later concealed and denied.

### The Iron Path
In the wake of the Heresy, the period known as the Scouring begins as the traitors flee Imperial justice. Iron Hands forces are drawn together on Medusa for the conclave known as the Tempering. This great council sets the Legion's feet on a path that it will follow, for better or worse, for the next ten thousand years.

# THE STEEL ENDURES

**For ten millennia since the Heresy's end, the Iron Hands have stood strong in the face of a hostile galaxy. However, the long, bloody years took their toll. In a war where the price of failure was racial annihilation, logic provided proof that no measure could be considered too extreme. Victory at all costs carried a price of its own – one that might yet prove insupportable.**

In the wake of the Horus Heresy, the Imperium was a dismal, shattered thing. As the beauty and grandeur of the Imperial Palace had been burned black in the fires of betrayal, so great swathes of the Emperor's star-spanning realm had suffered a similar fate. The Master of Mankind was a broken husk, and his dream of unity erased forever. Yet for all this, the Imperium retained might enough to exact a bloody revenge upon its many foes. There could be no forgiveness for the crimes of the traitors – those who now ruled in the Emperor's name had neither the ability nor the desire to prevent a war of reciprocity. So began the time known in the histories of the Imperium as the Scouring.

This was a period of monumental violence, of confusion and darkness. Though the newly founded Inquisition fought to root out corruption and expose wrong-doers to the cold light of Imperial justice, the galaxy's vast scope and dark, shadowed reaches worked against them. With new betrayals and cries for vengeance emerging daily, a great many bloody-handed deeds went unseen. The ravaged Space Marine Legions were no exception to this, with many striving to cover up their own misdemeanours or extract their pound of flesh from those who had wronged them. The Dark Angels, the Space Wolves, even the Ultramarines, all followed their own agendas as the wars of the Scouring gathered pace. The Iron Hands were no exception.

## THE TEMPERING

By the beginning of the thirty-first millennium, the Iron Council was fully established as the Iron Hands' ruling body. It now fell to them to direct the fate of their brothers, and to consider their Legion's greater purpose and responsibilities. While many Imperial factions bayed for blood and rushed to vent their fury upon those who had betrayed them, the Iron Hands gathered their strength on Medusa and convened the entire Iron Council in a conclave that would be known forever after as the Tempering. It went without saying that vengeance would be their first and greatest motivator, for their Legion had suffered more than any other during the bloodbath of the Heresy. Yet anger could not be allowed to rule, for by following such a path the mistakes of the Primarch would be repeated. Instead, the Iron Hands would have to calculate the most logical, measured course of action and follow it without remorse or division.

The debate ran long, days turning to weeks as all possible theories, doctrines and philosophies were discussed and dissected to an obsessive degree. Occasional outbursts of frustration or angry recriminations punctuated the discussion, each being met with universal disapproval and swift repression. The Primarch had bound the Iron Hands' wellspring of wrath in chains of discipline and expectation, and though his own emotions might have slipped their leash at the end, the Iron Hands could little afford to allow

the same thing to happen to them. Eventually, as the 86th Medusan day-cycle came to a close, the rulings of the Iron Council were announced and put into immediate effect. The Iron Fathers of the council had determined that it was the human race itself that was to blame for the Heresy. The Warmaster's rebellion had gained such traction only because the Space Marine Legions, the Primarchs, even the Emperor himself, were unable to eliminate human inconsistency from their decisions. Jealousy, avarice, fear – all were suppurating sores upon the human soul that must be seared clean in the fires of war. Trust, too, had played its part, for it was the Primarchs' trust in one another that had left the Imperium open to the abuses it had suffered. Those guilty of such weakness, the traitors and renegades who had fallen into rebellion, could not be allowed to spread their corruption to others. Humanity must be purged of its flaws in a war unending, lest that same weakness be allowed to take root once more.

So it was that the Iron Hands determined their guiding mission. They would extract payment for the wrongs done to them, but with a measured ruthlessness. In their every thought and deed, they would seek out weakness and destroy it, replacing it with the machine-like fortitude that they so venerated. The clan companies took ship that night, forged into unstoppable strike forces and distributed against the most appropriate foes as determined by pure logic. This was the beginning of a bloody campaign that would see the Iron Hands tested to the very limits of their endurance.

## THE VOICE OF MARS

*Unbeknownst to the wider Imperium, the Tempering also played host to several Adeptus Mechanicus envoys – with their Primarch lost, the Iron Fathers sought new strength to add to their own. The Priesthood of Mars and their Titan Legions had long fought beside the Iron Hands during the days of the Great Crusade and the Heresy alike, forging ever stronger bonds as they did so. In the devotees of the Omnissiah, the Iron Hands saw a mirror of their own doctrine of steel over flesh, a reliable ally who would not fall prey to hubris and pride as had the preening braggarts of the Emperor's Children. The Iron Council thus deemed it logical to offer the Adeptus Mechanicus closer military ties than ever before. In exchange for the Iron Hands' alliance and protection, the Martian Priesthood would grant them unprecedented access to the sacred mysteries of the Omnissiah, augmenting their Techmarines' knowledge far beyond that possessed by their counterparts in the other Legions of the Adeptus Astartes. By the Tempering's end, the Voice of Mars would be ratified as an official position upon the Iron Council itself, and would be occupied evermore by a triad of senior Tech-Adepts.*

# WAR UNENDING

In the wake of the decrees laid down during the Tempering and the division of the Second Founding, Clan Company Raukaan were ever at the forefront of the Iron Hands' wars. Their reputation for aggression stemmed from the days when Clan Raukaan of old had plied the Medusan wastes as piratical raiders. The next ten thousand years would see Clan Raukaan plunged into the fires of war more than any other company. However, several of these bloody campaigns formed ominous portents of things to come.

In the last years of M31, Clan Raukaan was deployed wholesale into the Ulmetrican Reach. Supported by elements of Clan Companies Avernii and Dorrvok and led by a cabal of no fewer than four Iron Fathers, this massive force was charged with crushing the rebellious factions that had spread throughout the system. What had begun as a workers' uprising on the factory moon of Tholsh had spread through the reach like wildfire, swiftly taking on alarming overtones of proscribed worship and fanaticism. Yet when the Iron Hands translated from the Warp to begin their war they found that their foe was cunning enough to evade open battle. Rather than stage full-scale armed rebellions, the cults were remaining well underground. They used powerful psykers to communicate with one another, and to influence the governors of the worlds they had infested. Initially, Iron Captain Morlus commanded his forces to strike with surgical precision – the Scouts of Clan Dorrvok were deployed on key worlds throughout the reach, sweeping mile by mile with machine-like patience in their search for cultist cells. As each such canker was located, teleport attacks and Drop Pod assault were used to bring massive force to bear and exterminate it completely. Yet almost a year of this approach seemed to bring the Iron Hands no closer to victory, the foe's numbers still unguessable. Repeatedly, the bravest Cultists used makeshift anti-orbital missiles to strike at Clan Company Raukaan's ships, each attack causing little damage but serving to goad the Iron Hands' buried anger a little closer to the surface. With no clear enemy to confront en masse, the majority of Clan Raukaan could do little but train, run drills, and wait for an opportunity to deploy.

Matters came to a head when, on the swamp-choked hive world of Pulus, several corrupt shrines were discovered by Clan Dorrvok's scouts. These foul, fleshy monuments gave praise to a Slaaneshi Daemon, named by its devoted worshippers as the Sapphire King. From that moment, the entire character of the war in the Ulmetrican Reach changed. The Iron Fathers met in conclave and determined that, by the core tenets of their Chapter and according to the decrees of the Tempering, they had no choice but to declare the entire populace of the reach guilty of the same brand of perversion that had twisted Fulgrim's Legion against them during the Heresy. That the vast majority of the reach's populace were not deemed directly responsible was neither here nor there – these supposed innocents had allowed a foul cancer to take root in their midst, and must be punished accordingly.

With a single command, the Iron Fathers unleashed the full might of their strike force against the worlds of the reach. In a war of extermination that took six years to conclude, the Iron Hands cleansed the taint of Slaanesh from the Ulmetrican Reach by the expedient of system-wide genocide. It was, after all, the most direct method of ensuring success.

## FAULTLESS SERVICE

As the centuries wore on, the Iron Hands were instrumental time and again in protecting the interests of the Imperium. If their conduct became ever less humane, few would have deemed their callous conduct to be a fault. During M34, the horrific phenomenon known as the Pale Wasting swept into the galaxy, great swarms of refugees and intergalactic flotsam fleeing before its miasmic grasp. Raukaan were among several clan companies who sent forces at the request of Mars, to ensure compliance with the quarantine cordon around the forge world of Grammachus Beta. For long months, the Iron Hands' Strike Cruisers hung in space, silent sentinels watching for any who might attempt to flee ahead of the Wasting and thus endanger the forge world or its output. Warriors of Raukaan, Kaargul and Haarmek performed brutal boarding actions against the craft of Ork raiders and Eldar pirates alike, sweeping them deck by deck with bolter and blade. As each ship was cleared, the corpses of their luckless inhabitants were catalogued, piled in heaps, and burned. The ships themselves were scuttled before being redirected into the heart of Gau-X24, the nearest star.

None remarked upon the fact that the same treatment was meted out upon the luckless Yormethi 26th Imperial Guard. An entire army group, the Yormethi had been charged with holding the Phorox Corridor. After misinterpreting their garbled orders, the Yormethi had retreated to join the cordon around Grammachus Beta. When their hails – and then their panicked pleas – went unanswered by the Iron Hands' ships, the Yormethi attempted to fight, but they were caught while still translating from the Warp. Their ships were bracketed by fire-patterns so efficient that thousands of men died without ever knowing who had killed them. For the remainder, there was nothing but the terrified wait aboard crippled ships, followed by a shockingly violent death under the guns of Iron Hands boarding parties. There could be no mercy for men who failed to remain at their posts, and so the Iron Hands gave them none.

During the dark days of the Moirae Schism in M35, great swathes of the Adeptus Mechanicus and their closest allies were riven with internal rebellion. The Iron Hands were not immune to this time of strife. Clan Raukaan was notable during this time of conflict for holding staunchly to their Chapter's core beliefs. Under the influence of Iron Chaplain Furnous and Iron Captain Hekkan, they were one of the only clan companies to have not a single battle-brother become corrupted by the pernicious Moirae doctrine; indeed, they deployed several squadrons of Vindicators and

Predators against rebellious Cataphractii forces during the battle of Kamjada. That these Adeptus Mechanicus rebels were supported by a small cadre of warriors from Clan Borrgos would form a point of bitter contention between the two clan companies for many centuries to come.

## A SHOW OF FORCE

In M37, the Iron Council made show of dispatching a huge force to aid in battle against the renegade disciples of the Blind King. Clan Raukaan and no fewer than four other clan companies took the field. In a series of bloody battles, their vast strike force blunted a dozen uprisings on as many worlds. At Pelos they even hurled back the turncoat Titans of the Legio Coventia with a vast armoured phalanx. As the war ground on, the Iron Hands were lauded as heroes by Segmentum Command and the Martian Priesthood alike.

However, this overt display of force concealed many months of doctrinal wrangling within the Iron Council themselves, some of whom had argued relentlessly that the renegade Tech-Priests of the Occlusiad – who believed the infinitely corruptible and imperfect human race to be an affront to the Omnissiah – might not be entirely in the wrong. Clan Raukaan's current Iron Father, the venerable Techmarine Daarmos, was amongst the loudest voice in shouting down these pernicious whispers for the madness they were. Raukaan's forces found themselves in the forefront of the conflict that followed. Yet it was under Daarmos' patronage that, less than two hundred years later, Clan Raukaan suffered one of their greatest defeats.

In the latter years of M40, after a string of brutal battles in the Myrmidia system against the Orks of Waaagh! Skullsmasha, Clan Raukaan received a distress call from the

### THE SIMULUS CHAMBERS

*The warships of the Iron Hands are significantly more complex than those of most other Chapters. They mount exceptionally high-yield weaponry powered by castigatus-class generators. They are sheathed in dense envelopes of autosanctified void shields and boast machine spirits capable of effecting their own repairs, not to mention directing combat operations independent of their crews. Yet arguably the Chapter's most valuable – and potentially controversial – devices are their simulus chambers. Standing in humming banks along the walls of the ships' conditioning decks, each simulus chamber comprises a harness-throne similar to those found in Drop Pods, lit with flickering blue electro-candles and recessed into an ornately frescoed alcove. When a battle-brother is strapped into the chamber's throne, neural plugs engage at the base of the spine and plunge the user into a trance-like state in which massive quantities of data can be inloaded or exloaded. The battle-brother's mind can be stimulated to provide artificial combat scenarios or conduct super efficient debriefs. Further, subconscious strategic protocols can be uploaded to prepare the Space Marine for any eventuality it has been predicted that he may face in the field. Some clan companies make greater use of these devices than other, Clan Garrsak in particular being renowned for performing every mission-briefing and war-council purely by simulus communion.*

Mars-class freighter *Endymion*, deep in the neighbouring Corladian Gulf. This cry for help reported an attack by traitors identified as the Emperor's Children and, more galling still, made mention of fanatical broadcasts claiming the souls of the ship's crew in the name of the Sapphire King. Iron Captain Maklon and Techmarine Daarmos were quick to respond, leaving a token force to keep watch for the Orks and taking a complement of more than half of Clan Raukaan's battle-brothers in search of the Traitors.

## DISASTER STRIKES

The Iron Hands strike force reached the last known coordinates of the *Endymion* to find the craft gone. However, localised scans quickly revealed a tangle of Warp signatures leading to the nearby death world of Skarvus. Led by Maklon and Daarmos, the warriors of Clan Raukaan made planetfall amid Skarvus' jagged bone-jungles. Thunderhawks descended to disgorge a sizeable armoured strike force. Their rumbling battle tanks and transports crunched through vast drifts of bonemeal and ploughed down calcified groves amid lashing squalls of flayer-hail, following the Warp signatures to their source.

Even as the vast, blazing carcass of the *Endymion* appeared on the horizon, sprawled and broken at the end of a twenty-mile trench, the traitors struck. Sonic weapons howled over the roar of engines, armour plates buckled and tracks sheared as oscillating waves of force tore them apart. Clan Raukaan fought back hard, overlapping fields of fire ensuring the optimum kill-ratio as the traitors advanced. Gaudily coloured figures in freakish armour were blown apart by ruby lances of energy and thudding barrages of mass-reactive shells. Bolters roared and grav-guns pounded the bonejungle flat. Yet the Emperor's Children outnumbered the Iron Hands several times over, and their well-executed ambush had lent them the element of surprise. Gradually the tanks and warriors of Clan Raukaan were torn apart by lethal sonic bombardments, fireballs blooming and bone trunks lit with the dancing light of white-hot fires.

Only a fraction of Maklon and Daarmos' forces escaped the ambush on Skarvus alive. Both of Raukaan's long-serving Iron Fathers had been lost in the disastrous battle, refusing to order the retreat even though they faced impossible odds. Worse still, while the Iron Hands' attention had been drawn away by the servants of the Sapphire King, the Orks had returned to Myrmidia in even greater numbers, as though they had known the system's defenders would be elsewhere. The ensuing carnage was a blow to the reputation of the Iron Hands as a whole, for a Chapter whose brethren chose to abandon their posts in order to chase old vendettas must be carefully watched. Clan Company Raukaan – their numbers much reduced and their battle-brothers facing the strictest censure – were placed under the command of the staunchly conservative Iron Father Kristos, a Techmarine of the old guard who was charged with ensuring no traces of Maklon or Daarmos' shortcomings remained. As the 41st Millennium dawned, Clan Company Raukaan was far from their Chapter's favour, yet still darker days lay ahead.

# FIRST AMONGST BROTHERS

The battle-brothers of Clan Company Raukaan have long been seen as dangerously unpredictable by many of their brethren. On numerous occasions, many on the Iron Council have accused Clan Raukaan of abandoning logic in favour of such sub-optimal motivators as anger or, worse, compassion. Yet their aggressive tendencies have served them well over the centuries, with every defeat being offset by numerous victories and the destruction of many terrible foes. Clan Raukaan's Hall of Conquest is heavy with ironglass plaques that proclaim deeds of honour and heroism, and amongst them are mentioned certain bands of warriors who have distinguished themselves in the service of the Imperium and their Chapter.

## TACTICAL SQUAD RIIS (2ND SQUAD)

Tactical Squad Riis have a well-earned reputation for fighting at the very forefront of every battle they join. The most accomplished drop-assault specialists in the entire clan company, Squad Riis exceed even some of Clan Raukaan's Assault Squads with the fervour of their attacks. This is due in large part to the bellicose nature of the battle-brothers that make up the squad. Their brother sergeant is a wrathful warrior whose minimalist augmetics and readily expressed emotions mark him as a zealous devotee of Kardan Stronos. The rest of Squad Riis are little different, renowned for their excess of choler and fury. On occasion, this outlook has led them to censure, even within the ranks of Clan Raukaan. Yet each time they surge from their Drop Pod into the heart of the foe with their boltguns blazing, Tactical Squad Riis reap a fearsome tally of the foe.

## TACTICAL SQUAD KALAG (5TH SQUAD)

The warriors of Tactical Squad Kalag are notorious for their methodical efficiency, even in the face of overwhelming enemy numbers. The other squads of the clan company claim that the battle-brothers of Kalag never waste a single shot, their exceptional fire control subroutines ensuring that every bolt finds its optimum mark in the body of a foe. Behind this dispassionate, mechanical mask, though, the battle-brothers of Squad Kalag conceal their own brand of cold, vehement hatred. It is a mark of pride amongst the squad that no member of Kalag will ever take a single step backward, and their multitude of bionic augmentations are testament to the toll paid for their stubbornness. In battle, Squad Kalag will refuse to give ground no matter how great the enemy's numbers or how hopeless the situation may appear.

## ASSAULT SQUAD NEIM (7TH SQUAD)

Assault Squad Neim have become expert in the support and optimization of Clan Raukaan's armoured offensives. Whenever the clan company's tanks or Dreadnoughts are deployed en masse, the battle-brothers of Neim go to war alongside them. To this end, they have trained relentlessly in the art of fighting in concert with such potent engines of war. They can spot and exploit a breakthrough the moment it occurs, can read the intentions of a tank's machine spirit through subtle nuances of code-bleed and weapon orientation, and are experts at timing their counter-attacks to intercept potential infantry threats to a vehicle's vulnerable flanks and rear. At the battle of Broken Hopes, Squad Neim even formed an informal honour guard for Venerable Furnous. Several battle-brothers gave their lives to protect the mighty Dreadnought before the fighting was done, and were honoured with interment into Dreadnought sarcophagi of their own after the war's end.

## DEVASTATOR SQUAD SELOX (9TH SQUAD)

Referred to unofficially as 'Ferrus' Vengeance', Devastator Squad Selox are well known for their ability to record, catalogue and maintain a grievance almost indefinitely. Though their target prioritisation protocols never show overt signs of being overridden, and their battlefield effectiveness remains within optimal parameters, Squad Selox will always seize an opportunity to avenge an old slight when on campaign. Time and again, their battle-brothers have been heard to identify heretic war engines or monstrous horrors as perpetrators of some previous atrocity against the Chapter or the Imperium, these fell deeds sometimes dating from hundreds of years in the past. Once their identities have been confirmed by Squad Selox's merciless marksmen, these foes will be targeted with extreme detestation, fired upon to the exclusion of all else until they are reduced to flaming ruin.

# SLAUGHTER ON DAWNBREAK

**For Clan Company Raukaan, the first years of Kristos' command were a brutal grind. The losses they had suffered on Skarvus were steadily replenished with reserves from Clan Companies Borrgos and Morlaag, bringing Raukaan back toward full battle readiness. Yet it was not the clan company's numerical strength that was in question.**

Iron Father Kristos was charged with running a full program of 'analytical redemption', working from Raukaan's command structure downward. Kristos, a Techmarine of some one hundred and eighty years and a long-standing Iron Father, embodied the inhumanity that so many of his Chapter had now embraced. A looming warrior-engineer whose armour concealed a body more than eighty percent augmetic, Kristos had made numerous pilgrimages to the forges of Mars during his life. He was a creature of the Omnissiah's doctrines through and through, seemingly bereft of emotion, compassion or empathy. On his recommendation, the fallen Iron Captain Maklon was replaced by the relentlessly logical Iron Captain Graevaar, who immediately instigated a regime of additional psycho-conditioning throughout Clan Raukaan. Squad by squad, the clan company's battle-brothers marched to the conditioning decks, there to submit to long, painful months of cerebral recohesion – this was intended to smother any lingering traces of emotional attachment to the company's previous Iron Fathers and their questionable methods. Preparatory missions were undertaken, the clan company tested methodically – component by component – to ensure no signs of weakness remained.

Decades passed in minor engagements and support duties before Iron Captain Graevaar and his Techmarine comrade were satisfied with the battle-readiness of their clan company. Kristos returned to the Iron Council and reported Raukaan once again ready for front-line combat operations. Amid a general rumble of approval from his peers, Kristos was charged with a new mission that would serve to 'field-test' Clan Raukaan's iron hard discipline and merciless conditioning. The Voice of Mars had advised the Iron Council of a distress call received by an Adeptus Mechanicus listening post, a signal that had proved most interesting.

## PARADISE BURNS

Some weeks later, a combined force of battle-brothers from Clans Raukaan, Avernii, Dorrvok and Garrsak burst from the Warp into the Aebrasyn System. Iron Hands tactical doctrine espouses the deployment of overwhelming strength in all things. The force calculated appropriate for the mission at hand was thus sufficient to crush a star system beneath its armoured tread. As the Iron Hands' augurs came online, they detected hails from other Imperial forces, namely the Catachan 17th Army Group already arrayed on and around the massive garden world of Dawnbreak. The Catachans had been deployed some months earlier, responding to the same astropathic message from the world's noble inhabitants that had reached the Adeptus Mechanicus.

For several hundred years, Dawnbreak had been cultivated as a retreat for those privileged few among the Administratum and Ministorum given permission to settle

there. Silver city-spires climbed into the heavens, rising from amid a lush arboreal ocean that covered two thirds of the planet's surface. Yet the sculpted shrinegardens and glittering retreats of Dawnbreak had come under sudden, violent attack from xenos raiders identified as the Eldar of Craftworld Alaitoc. The attack had come after labour-teams, excavating a site for a new system of ornamental cave-gardens, had discovered strange machineries buried dormant beneath the planet's crust. How the Eldar could have known this, or why it might goad them to such violence was beyond the planet's governor. Nonetheless, the Eldar had come, striking first at the dig site and then working outward in what appeared to be a systematic purge of human life. The Catachans had been sent by Segmentum Command to rescue the noble worthies who called Dawnbreak their home. Yet far from disappearing like smoke – as the Eldar are wont to do – the arrival of the Catachan forces only seemed to spur the foe to greater efforts. Vast swathes of Dawnbreak's forests had burned, crystalline domes and looming arch-templums falling in fire and ruin, and the Catachans in turn had called for help.

The Iron Hands moved in-system, swiftly closing on Dawnbreak and adopting optimal orbital positioning. They released swarms of clicking, buzzing servo-skulls into the upper atmosphere, the macabre servitors spreading across the globe to perform strategic divinations and weave a sensor-tapestry of force dispositions and strategic movements. Responding to Catachan General Dortmund's hails with only the most perfunctory code-bursts, the strike force's Iron Fathers held a holoconclave to determine their strategy. They had detected no xenos craft in orbit, though they did not discount the possibility of such ships lurking somewhere beyond sensor-range. For the time being, however, the Eldar possessed nothing in the way of orbital support. Their ground forces, meanwhile, seemed to be well dispersed. Formed into highly mobile airborne battle groups, they were performing a graceful dance of destruction as they picked off one human enclave after another with near impunity.

The Imperial Guard had concentrated their forces around the greatest of these sites, adopting a typically static defence and attempting to evacuate outlying civilian elements to these supposed saviour-zones. None of this held any interest for Kristos or his comrades. Chasing shadows and smoke through the vast forests of Dawnbreak was not the way the Iron Hands made war, while if the Imperial Guard and civilian forces were unable to save themselves then they did not deserve the Iron Hands' assistance anyway. The Iron Fathers had eyes only for the dig-site, and the substantial Eldar forces that held it. Here was the discovery that had prompted the attack on Dawnbreak, and here the Iron Hands would strike.

## IRON RAIN

The midday sun filtered down through rolling banks of smoke, dappling the churned mud and wrecked machinery of the dig site with drifting patterns as the Iron Hands launched their attack. The birds fell suddenly silent amid the trees, and bands of blue-armoured Eldar sentries snapped their gaze skyward. A second later the clouds tore open. The watery rays of the sun were replaced by screaming columns of devastating laser energy and plummeting bombardment cannon shells. Great swathes of forest were blasted to ash in an instant, exploding in monstrous eruptions of tumbling earth, pulped undergrowth and mangled bodies. As the suppression fire rolled steadily outwards from the dig site, the blazing contrails of Drop Pods filled the skies. Iron Hands aircraft wove between them, their calculated flight paths carrying them through the plummeting ordnance and drop-craft with perfect synchronicity. Eldar warriors dashed for cover amid the ruined buildings dotting the site or fell back into the yawning crater at its heart as the black-hulled Drop Pods slammed down and began to disgorge squad after squad of armoured battle-brothers.

Clan Raukaan had the lead, stepping from their harnesses with measured strides and forming cold, efficient ranks. As they initiated their lockstep advance, Eldar fire began to lash out at them from all around, beams of white light and hissing shuriken rounds battering the Marines' armour. Here and there, battle-brothers stumbled to the ground or were vaporised by energy blasts, yet Clan Raukaan's warriors advanced with an inexorable, fearless tread,

loosing the furious thunder of their guns as they did so. Fragile xenos bodies exploded in bursts of blood and gore, while a screaming squadron of jetbikes was punched from the sky by the relentless storm of fire amid blossoms of flame and sparks. As the warriors of Clan Raukaan pushed forward, more Drop Pods slammed down amid their lines, disgorging roaring Dreadnoughts that swiftly added their massive firepower to the fusillade. Elsewhere, Thunderhawk Gunships and Transporters disgorged squadrons of black-armoured battle tanks, their engines gunning furiously as they surged toward the foe.

## INTENSIFIED HOSTILITIES

The Eldar fought back with everything they had, skimming grav-tanks rising from the dig crater to direct lethal volleys of fire into the advancing Space Marines. Long-barrelled laser cannons and strange crystalline guns spat death, blowing more Iron Hands off their feet. The Dreadnought that had once been Iron Chaplain Furnous reeled as a beam of energy punched through his sarcophagus and crippled his servo-motors. Yet even as the mighty ancient fought to reroute motive power past his damaged systems, he felt the cold presence of strange machine spirits questing through his metal body, repairing damage and blessing him once more with the power to walk. As he strode forward with fresh vigour, Furnous detected the presence of Iron Father Kristos nearby, the Ironstone mag-clamped around his neck. A potent relic of the Chapter, this silvered pendant was reputedly haunted by ancient and powerful machine spirits, capable of bolstering the failing strength of the machines around them.

Kristos advanced amid a phalanx of Land Raiders and Predators that the enemy's fire proved unable to stop. Around Kristos and his lumbering Servitor bodyguards, the tanks of Clan Raukaan soaked up blasts of coruscating energy and hammering beams of light, their tracks churning on and their guns continuing to roar regardless. Gaping rents were torn in the vehicles' armour, weapon systems were crippled and drives burst into flame. Each time, though, the tanks lurched to life once more before the eyes of the increasingly desperate Eldar, damage that would have overcome even the sophisticated machine spirits of the Iron Hands repaired by the Ironstone's influence.

Storms of psychic lightning leapt from the hands of Eldar seers now emerging from the crater into the very teeth of Clan Raukaan's assault. Around them, Aspect Warriors charged forward in brightly patterned war-plate. At the same moment, risking the fury of the ongoing bombardment as they bounded through the trees, a pair of towering Wraithknights took to the field, surrounding the warriors of the Iron Hands. Their guns carved bloody furrows through Clan Raukaan's lines, yet even this was not enough. Stormraven Gunships struck from the smoke, missiles shrieking from their wings to explode against the Wraithknights' statuesque bodies while the Terminators of Clan Avernii charged toward them with thunder hammers held high. As the battle raged to the rear, Iron Father Kristos and Iron Captain Graevaar led a final push on the crater.

Psychic lightning lashed at Graevaar as he charged toward the Eldar witches, the energy dancing across his augmetic limbs and crackling over his steel-plated skull. With a roar of defiance he kept going, even as his skin crisped and curled like parchment, swinging his silvered blade in a mighty arc and sending the head of the foremost seer tumbling away over the lip of the crater. A cry of dismay went up from the Eldar at this sight, swiftly drowned out once more by the thunder of Clan Raukaan's boltguns. One by one, the broken corpses of the Eldar warriors were sent tumbling into the pit, and the sound of gunfire was replaced by rumbling tracks and marching feet as the Iron Hands consolidated their hold on their true objective with blank efficiency.

In the wake of the Iron Hands' assault, the war for Dawnbreak continued to rage. The Eldar had lost their leader and their purpose, yet they dared not try to strike at the massive concentration of Iron Hands who held the dig site. However, outraged calls for assistance from the Catachan soldiery continued to fall on deaf ears as the Iron Fathers went about their business. For long days, patrols of Iron Hands swept the broken wasteland that surrounded the dig site, armoured columns that travelled in force and crushed any foe they encountered. Though the Eldar made several more attempts to dislodge the Space Marines, these attacks lacked for numbers and conviction. They were swiftly crushed. Meanwhile, under the icy glare of massive lumen-fonts, heavy duty Servitors worked tirelessly. They expanded upon the excavations started by the civilian dig-teams, widening the shafts and ponderously dragging their prize to the surface, one segment at a time. Thunderhawk Transporters ferried shrouded cargoes into space, working day and night to complete their work. In all this time, however, the Iron Hands never strayed from the dig site. The Catachans' calls for aid went unanswered. Civilian vox-hails were ignored. The Iron Fathers who led the expedition had no interest in aiding their supposed allies, and wasted neither time or resource intervening in their plight.

As the Catachans began to realise these Space Marines were not quite the reinforcements they had hoped for, morale in the ranks plunged. The Eldar were still performing hit and run raids across the planet, instigating savage battles that now had the character of revenge attacks. Suddenly, one morning, the Iron Hands were simply gone. General Dortmund raged over the vox-link as recovery craft descended to ferry the mighty Iron Hands force back to orbit and the Space Marine fleet made ready to depart. Even when a fleet suspected to be made up of Eldar ships appeared on outsystem augurs – coming to rescue their remaining comrades and avenge their leader's death – the Iron Hands proceeded regardless and the Catachan shouts turned to desperate pleas for rescue. As the Iron Hands ships burned retros and set a course for home, Dortmund received a single vox-response from Iron Captain Graevaar.

'If you are strong you will survive. If you are weak you will not. Fight hard, General, and prove your worth.'

*Autarch Yeldrian of Craftworld Alaitoc strode across the scorched earth of the battlefield, his every movement speaking of the anger he felt. Eldar bodies were being collected one by one, their precious remains bound for Vampire Raiders that would return them to orbit. Many had lain for days, left piled in the mud where they had been slain. The spirit stones of some still flickered with life, yet others were disturbingly dark, as dead as the bodies that rotted beneath them.*

*Here and there amid the Eldar fallen lay the shattered carcasses of black-armoured, post-human warriors, their chests and throats ripped open by some kind of grotesque surgery. These Space Marines were not like others Yeldrian had encountered – those had been the red-armoured brethren of the Blood Angels, noble warriors alongside whom the Autarch had briefly fought against a common foe. He had felt, if not respect, then at least a certain warrior kinship with those primitive heroes.*

*These Space Marines though, these were a different breed. Lumpen mechanical arms and legs were much in evidence, cumbersome prosthetics which appeared to Yeldrian nought but a clumsy encumbrance. These black-armoured savages had left their lesser human allies to die, allowing their ships to be torn apart by the guns of Yeldrian's vengeful fleet. None had survived, and the wreckage of the primitive spaceships was still raining down on the doomed world. The remaining Imperial forces on the ground had been slain in their turn, yet even now Yeldrian felt no sense of victory, just aching loss and fury.*

*Farseer Elmath was dead along with so many of Alaitoc's brave warriors, and the Autarch already knew what he would find when he reached the crater's lip. Some secrets should stay buried, he thought, for much of the galaxy's knowledge was too dangerous to be revealed to the lesser, younger races. Yet sure enough, as his gaze swept the deep pit that the humans had dug, Yeldrian felt despair pressing on his heart. These black-armoured Space Marines, whoever or whatever they were, had stolen the old treasures of those who should never be woken...*

# THE BATTLE FOR COLUMNUS

**In the wake of their assault upon Dawnbreak, Clan Company Raukaan once again enjoyed the full faith of the Iron Council. Kristos and Graevaar had done their work well, it seemed, restoring the purity of logic to Raukaan's warriors.**

Upon the Dawnbreak expedition's return to Medusa, the recovered xenos machineries were consigned to vaults deep underground and their fate commented upon no further. Meanwhile, Clan Company Raukaan was reinstated to full front-line duties. The decades that followed saw them victorious time and again under the continuing leadership of Iron Father Kristos and Iron Captain Graevaar – now an honoured Iron Father in his own right. It was nearly two hundred years after the victory on Dawnbreak that word reached the Iron Council of the plight of Columnus. A venerable forge world on the western fringe of Segmentum Solar, Columnus sat directly in the path of a vast Ork Waaagh! Even now, the xenos were flowing toward Columnus like a huge wave, depopulating outlying systems and sweeping the scattered Imperial defenders before them like flotsam on the tide. The forge world's senior magi had requested immediate aid, and the Iron Hands would give it.

Less than a month after the distress call had been received, a mighty fleet of black-hulled ships hove into orbit above Columnus, each bearing the white gauntlet of the Iron Hands upon its flanks. Over a third of the Chapter's strength had been deployed – no fewer than ten Iron Fathers led this expedition, commanding a force that included the whole of Clans Raukaan and Garrsak as well as representative forces from almost every other clan company. As the Iron Hands' helm-servitors established vox-links with the defenders on Columnus, the Iron Hands learned that they would be fighting in good company. The entirety of the Legio Ferrax had been assembled, the 'Iron Wolves' boasting over thirty

## IRON OVER FLESH

*The Iron Hands make extensive use of bionics and augmetics, far more so than any other Chapter. Their vehicle crews plug directly into their tanks using mind interface uplinks similar to those found in Titans, kneeling in direct communion with the machine spirits that serve them. Where many Chapters employ serfs or thralls, the Iron Hands use a vast range of servitors, from bulky units charged with carrying and supplying ammunition to dextrous and spindle-limbed cyborgs whose duty it is to affect repairs to the tangled inner workings of the Iron Hands' spacecraft. Even the apothecarions aboard the Iron Hands' fleet have the look of machine-shops – great racks of augmetic limbs, organs and systems hang from their walls ready for implantation, while Apothecaries and Techmarines combine their talents in order to restore their patients' bodies to optimum efficiency and strength.*

Titans of varying classes. Phalanx upon phalanx of Skitarii, Cataphractii and augmented tech-guard garrisoned the sprawling, city-sized fortress factories that dotted Columnus. Dozens of regiments of Imperial Guard tanks, artillery and super-heavy armour had been assembled on the planet's crimson plains, or held the raised super-highways that connected one fortress factory with the next. Countless guns pointed skyward, waiting for the Orks' assault, and the Iron Hands moved quickly to add their own. As the Orks' landing sites were likely to be both random and numerous, it was deemed that the Iron Hands' strength must remain as concentrated as was practical. The Iron Fathers thus split their force into three company-sized armies, and deployed them to the greatest of the fortress factories – Kemlos, Urdri and Slartav. Yet as the tanks of Clan Raukaan roared up the highway toward Urdri, Kristos and Graevaar were to receive disturbing news. The Iron Hands were not the only Space Marines present in defence of Columnus.

As the warriors of Clan Raukaan began moving to their posts within the labyrinthine factory-sprawl of Urdri, Shadow Captain Stenn of the Raven Guard approached them. Accompanied by his command squad, Stenn extended the Iron Hands' commanders a greeting and offer of brotherhood. He explained that his force had been effecting a fighting retreat before the oncoming Orks to slow their advance, giving the defenders of Columnus time to prepare. Now Stenn's men were ready to fight in earnest, and he possessed important information regarding the peculiar strengths of the foe. In response, Kristos' silence stretched long, growing ever more uncomfortable as his augmetics hissed and whirred. Finally the Techmarine replied.

'The Raven Guard cannot be relied upon,' he announced in buzzing tones. 'You fight like smoke, drifting away in the slightest breeze. Additional: Orks are no new foe to the Iron Hands, you know nothing that our battle simulations have not already told us. We will not fight alongside you, Shadow Captain Stenn, for it is in all we do as Iron Hands to avoid the fate suffered by our Primarch.' The Iron Father and his men swept past the bristling Raven Guard, the crash of their boots receding as they made for their command-post.

The Orks arrived scant days later, and their fury was a thing to behold. The Astropaths had been wailing for hours, many dying in the grip of convulsions so severe that they broke their necks or chewed off their own tongues. As each psyker perished, the Tech Adepts of the Colosseum Astropathica simply unlocked another from stasis storage, yet the Astropaths were dying as fast as they could be plugged back into their thrones. Now, as the Orks' enormous fleet appeared above Columnus, an almighty surge of psionic energy rolled out from amid the greenskin armada. As the bow-wave struck home, every single surviving Astropath died at once in a blaze of green flame that consumed the Colosseum, leaving nothing but a glowing crater in its wake.

## THE BEAST DESCENDS

Even as the bodies of Columnus' first fallen were blazing in the wreckage, orbital augurs were attempting to calculate the size of the greenskin armada descending upon the planet. The Ork ships resembled a meteor storm of incredible density. Rocket-propelled asteroids and tumbling, thruster-studded lumps of metal jostled for space with snub-nosed attack ships that belched trails of black smoke into the void as they passed. Ploughing through the mass like predatory beasts came slab-sided capital ships, each a preposterous tangle of armour and guns. Worst of all, at the fleet's heart loomed a mighty space hulk the size of a small moon. Around it played a weird halo of green lightning, alike to a storm in space. This was Waaagh! Zagdakka, and it descended upon Columnus at breakneck speed.

The orbital fortresses were the first to feel the Orks' wrath. Forge worlds are repositories of the most ancient and deadly technologies, and Columnus' orbitals were equipped with a vast array of weapons systems. Strobing webs of high-powered lasers reached out into the void, cutting through Ork ships to dissect them in seconds. Vortex warheads detonated amidst tightly packed clusters of greenskin craft and dragged them into the howling void. Gravity drivers crushed Ork ships to scrap or smashed them into one another with deadly force, while vast cycling batteries of missiles and lasers lit the skies of Columnus with their fury. The Orks simply accelerated, charging into the rain of fire.

Thousands of attack ships and ramming craft were blown apart, shattering into expanding clouds of fire and spinning debris, yet thousands remained. Having exploited the smaller craft as crude shields, the larger assault craft and cruisers now ploughed forward through the plummeting wreckage and opened up with weapons of their own. A ferocious firestorm tore the heavens from pole to pole. Missiles and explosive munitions filled the diminishing gap between the orbitals and their myriad aggressors, the curtain of fire and debris becoming so dense that it seemed nothing could survive it. Yet impossibly, as if driven by some will greater than their own, the Orks came on. Many of the larger asteroids simply ploughed through the incoming fire, their rocky 'hulls' absorbing impacts that would have annihilated more conventional craft.

Without slowing, they slammed into the orbital fortresses and ripped them apart. Proud bastions that had hung in space for millennia fragmented like shattered glass, explosions stitching through them and immolating their doomed garrisons. From the surface of Columnus it appeared as though the sky had caught fire, the planet's omnipresent smog banks shredding to reveal tumbling, blazing swathes of wreckage falling toward the surface. Amid this rain of metal and fire came the Orks, ploughing their crude ships down through the atmosphere without the slightest pause. All across the planet, defensive batteries and silos opened fire, desperate to destroy the steel rain before it hit. They would not succeed.

## A LOGICAL COURSE

Columnus writhed like a beast in pain. Tumbling agglomerations of wreckage the size of mountains crashed down upon fortified outposts and massed armies, obliterating all they struck. Swathes of Skitarii and Imperial Guardsmen were killed as the blast waves from each impact rolled outward. Super-heavy tanks were flung end over end, while Titans reeled and shook like men standing in the path of a gale. Firestorms howled around them, overloading their void shields one by one. It was madness, destruction and death on an unimaginable scale, and in its midst the Orks made planetfall. Asteroid ships gouged vast craters from Columnus' arid plains as they struck. Huge scrapmetal cruisers burned retros, or else were enfolded in skeins of shimmering green energy that seemed to slow their descent, skidding to a stop at the end of miles-long blazing trenches. Smaller craft fell all around them, skimming low on gravity cushions, lurching to a halt on flaming clouds of jetwash, or simply crashing headlong into the planet's surface at full speed. Many Orks were killed upon impact, yet millions remained to spill out from their landing sites onto Columnus' burning surface.

Now the war began in earnest. As the greenskin space hulk settled into low orbit and began to rain fire and drop-craft onto Columnus' surface, the Iron Hands' fleet moved to engage, dwarfed by their monstrous foe yet unwilling to show a moment's weakness. Around them, Mechanicus war barges and Imperial Navy battleships swept forward, adding their ordnance to the Iron Hands' own and lighting the skies with a fresh storm of fire. On the surface, meanwhile, the Iron Hands found themselves with no shortage of foes to engage. The fortress factories had been protected from the worst of the devastating bombardment by humming banks of void shields, yet elsewhere the forge world's defenders had been horribly mauled.

Whole regiments had been obliterated in moments, major forge complexes swept from the map or buried in blazing wreckage. The world's noosphere was clogged with crackling static and radioactive interference, yet cautious estimates by the senior Colomnite Technomagi suggested that as much as forty percent of their world's defensive strength had been lost at a stroke, wiped out or left so shattered and cut off as to be as good as dead. Now the plains were awash with xenos who moved with a single purpose, vast tides making straight for the fortress factories and evidencing none of the typical infighting that might be expected from the barbaric and fractious Orks. What such a thing could mean, the magi could not guess.

Superior systems meant the Iron Fathers had retained contact with one another where the other defenders had not, and they swiftly confirmed that all three primary fortress factories were within hours of being besieged. Already there were isolated warbands of greenskins loose within Kemlos, and millions more were on their way. It was agreed that, with so many of the lesser defenders removed from the equation, even the might of the Iron Hands and Titans present on Columnus could not hope to face the greenskins out in the open. While Iron Father Kristos reported that the Raven Guard had departed Urdri in order to harry the advancing Orks and gather survivors, the Iron Hands saw no valid reason to do the same. Thus it was decided – the three great fortress factories would be islands against which the Orks would break. All Iron Hands would remain within the bounds of the cities, and exterminate the Ork forces as they advanced into engagement range. All Imperial assets beyond the walls would be considered lost and no effort wasted in attempting to rescue those too weak to save themselves. Only when the greenskins had exhausted their strength by hurling wave after wave against the defences would the Iron Hands sally forth and crush what remained of the greenskin threat. It was a logical, pragmatic course of action and the Iron Fathers dispersed to prepare their forces.

Iron Hands battle-brothers marched to take positions on the fortress factories' walls, or mustered around pre-plotted kill-zones ready to repulse those xenos who broke through. Squadron upon squadron of black armoured battle tanks rumbled into position at key intersections, their crews communing directly with their machine spirits and ready for battle. Deep within the towering bastions at each city's heart, Chapter servitors lumbered across launch decks and skyshield pads, loading fuel and ordnance into waiting Stormtalon and Stormraven Gunships. Devastators and Centurions of Clans Raukaan and Vurgaan took up positions, synched their minds with their targeting augmetics, and readied their weapons for the arrival of the innumerable horde.

Servo-skulls swarmed above Urdri, streaming back what strategic auguries they could. Iron Fathers Kristos and Graevaar watched alongside the other command personnel of Clan Raukaan as patchy images reached them of seas of greenskins flowing toward the city. The invaders were moving up the south and east superhighways, and from all directions across the plains; a great mass of rumbling tanks, lumbering walkers and millions of charging infantry that raised dust-storms in their wake. Scattered Imperial forces retreated before them, two limping Reaver Titans of the Legio Ferrax backing steadily up the southern highway with their guns thundering. Meanwhile, a ragged column of armour was approaching from the east, fire-blackened Raven Guard transports hurtling along amid a mish-mash of Chimeras and Leman Russ.

In both cases, the Orks were close on the defenders' heels, threatening to overrun them at any moment, yet the Iron Hands had set their plans and combat protocols and they would not deviate. The desperate Imperial forces glanced up at the fortress walls as they pushed towards them, to see only an implacable line of silent black armour topping each.

Shields were dropped, gates rattled open and defensive batteries lit with fire as the warriors garrisoning Urdri provided an opening for the Titans and tanks to get into the city. Yet none sallied out to their aid; the retreating forces would have to rely on their own strength to reach safety, or fall. The Raven Guard and their wards hammered across the plains with Ork bikes and buggies nipping at their heels, greenskin aircraft screaming low overhead to drop bombs amid the fleeing tanks. A Rhino erupted in a blossom of fire, cartwheeling end over end as an Ork bomb struck it, and

the two rearmost Leman Russ went up in flames as crude energy weapons punched through their armour. Moments later, the surviving tanks were roaring through the gate while curtains of fire from Iron Hands and tech-guard slaughtered Orks in droves.

The Reavers were less fortunate. The venerable *Dictat Ferrum* was limping badly as it retreated, flames boiling from ragged tears in the armour of both legs. Even as the defenders watched from the walls, roiling green energy gathered above the heads of the advancing Orks like storm clouds. A mighty war-cry rose from countless throats, drifting feral and monstrous on the wind, and then the green energy leapt out to halo the *Ferrum*. The Titan's void shields imploded with a hollow thump as ectoplasmic energy roiled around them, and in a series of rippling explosions the Titan's weapons systems and ammunition reserves cooked off. With a thunderous boom, the *Dictat Ferrum* tumbled backwards, crashing bodily into her sister engine the *Sanctus Absolom* with tremendous force. Its balance destroyed, the second god-machine's war horn gave a forlorn howl of anguish as it too toppled from the raised highway to crash in ruin upon the plains below. As countless greenskins swarmed across the fallen Reavers, Gate 764 rumbled closed once more, shutting out Ork attackers and Imperial stragglers alike.

Now the defence of the city proper began. Time and again, surging tides of greenskins charged towards the walls, crude firepower blazing up from the ramshackle tanks that rumbled along in their midst. Each time, the charging Orks

were haloed with crackling green power, and refused to retreat no matter their losses. Yet each time, the rain of fire from the walls slaughtered every last greenskin before they could force a breach. Deep within the city, Clan Raukaan Whirlwinds and Hunters raised their weapons to the sky, the former pounding barrages of fire into the Orks beyond the walls while the latter added their skyspear missiles to the churning curtains of flak that the city's many turrets threw up against the screaming xenos aircraft.

For several hours the battle ground on, the battle-brothers of Clan Raukaan directing endless streams of bolter fire, missiles and grenades down into the seething horde beyond the walls as arms-servitors marched back and forth, keeping them supplied with a steady flow of ammunition. Though no answer could be found for the strange psychic phenomena displayed by the Orks, or their utter determination in the face of horrific casualties, mountainous drifts of greenskin corpses piled up amid blazing wrecks in their hundreds, and the combat readouts of the Iron Hands continued to show optimal results.

## THE WEIRDWAAAGH!

Had the Iron Hands listened to the council of Shadow Captain Stenn – who had been fighting this foe for many weeks – they would have better understood the threat they faced. Upon reaching the safety of the city, the Shadow Captain had made straight for the walls, spreading his men out to keep watch while repeatedly attempting to hail the Iron Fathers or senior magi of the city. Stenn was considering going to the Iron Hands commanders in person and forcing them to listen when suddenly, to the south of the city, a mighty green light flared. The time for warnings was done – the Weirdwaaagh! had arrived.

The Orks attacking Columnus were led by a mighty prophet of Mork, an enormous Weirdboy by the name of Zagdakka. So great were Zagdakka's powers that he had slain the previous Warlord, himself a great brute on an Ork, and taken the Waaagh! for his own, gathering about him every frothing Warphead he could get his glowy green hands on. This was his Weirdwaaagh! and like some bloated parasite, he used its powers to control the minds of his many followers. The fate of *Dictat Ferrum* had showed the signs of the Warpheads' work, but Stenn had been in no position to make sure.

Now, as a green tidal wave of Waaagh! energy hurtled across the plains and struck Urdri's wall, the Shadow Captain's worst fears were confirmed. The wall did not explode nor collapse. An entire section of the five hundred foot high, quarter-mile deep fortification simply glowed bright green for brief seconds before blinking out of existence, taking its defenders with it.

Immediately the vox-net erupted, horrified reports and frantic requests for confirmation shooting back and forth. Meanwhile, an almighty horde of greenskins surged into

---

## CALCULATED FORCE

*Even in the days before the Horus Heresy, the Iron Hands always believed that the best tactic was the methodically applied deployment of direct, overwhelming force. Since the Tempering, that doctrine has been taken to ever greater extremes. Desperate battles against the odds make little sense when Mankind faces a war for its very survival, and logic dictates that the Adeptus Astartes are one of the most precious resources at the Imperium's disposal. Surely then, that resource should not be hurled needlessly into fights that cannot be won.*

*Before each deployment, the Iron Council therefore performs an assessment known as the Calculum Rationale. All available information is taken into account, including current enemy strengths, availability of super-heavy or orbital assets, reinforcements, atmospheric conditions, and a thousand other factors of increasing obscurity. This assessment, when completed, states the exact number of battle-brothers, vehicles and supporting personnel required to ensure Imperial victory. If forces are available that match the projected sum, that exact amount of war material will be released by the Iron Council and expected to achieve a conclusive victory. No additional warriors will be sent, nor reinforcements provided should failure loom. Equally, if the Iron Hands do not possess the calculated number of readily available personnel to invest a war zone successfully, they will not do so. The annals of the Iron Council are replete with examples of worlds left to burn for the want of a single Stormtalon, Scout or boltgun.*

the gap left in Urdri's defences, more psychic blasts lashing out to lick at the walls as the xenos charged into the breach. Clipped orders rolled across the vox from the Iron Hands' officers, reserves of armour and infantry moving to plug the gap. Their implanted simulus subroutines contained no appropriate response to such an unpredictable threat. The Iron Hands froze stock-still for long seconds, twitching sporadically as subconsciously inculcated protocols jarred with reality. Slowly, they began to respond; Stormravens bearing Dreadnoughts and squads of Centurions toward the gap in the lines, but they would be too late.

Thus, as the first xenos scrambled through the breach, they were met by the Raven Guard. Black and white armoured Space Marines thumped along the walls, leaping into the air and driving themselves groundwards with blasts from their jump packs. As they dropped, bolt pistols flared and lightning claws lashed out, carving through swathes of Orks. The two forces crashed together, but the Raven Guard were few and the Orks all but numberless. With Zagdakka and his Weirdmob shoving their way toward the front, Stenn's forces could hold the foe back for minutes at best. The Shadow Captain laid about himself with his lightning claw, tearing an Ork's head from its shoulders before immolating two more with his plasma pistol. Around him, his men were fighting like heroes, blades and power fists dismembering greenskins with every swing. Yet the Orks seemed endless.

Stenn tried desperately to vox for support, or reach his Strike Cruiser in orbit. He was met with a squeal of feedback. Could the Orks be shrouding their vox? Then he saw them, drawing up in ordered ranks with their weapons ready, perhaps one hundred yards behind the breach. Iron Hands, dozens of them – battle-brothers and Centurions and Dreadnoughts and rumbling tanks all arrayed for war. They were watching impassively as the Orks overran Stenn's command one by one. At their head, surrounded by a cohort of mindless Gun Servitors, Iron Father Kristos leaned upon his power axe as he watched the Raven Guard die.

Stenn felt his wrath burn white hot as he realised that his men were being used as bait; his jump pack roared to life as he turned to hurl himself at the Iron Father. Yet at that moment searing green bolts of light exploded amid the battle, huge fists of ectoplasm scooping up Raven Guard and Orks alike and crushing them into paste. Stenn screamed with rage as crackling green tendrils wound around his limbs and spun him about, holding him up before an enormous Ork shaman, its eyes blazing behind a freakish scrap-metal mask. As the tendrils tightened, Stenn's armour began to fracture and spark. Blood spurted from between its plates as his bones cracked, and Stenn screamed as loud as he could.

'Damn you Kristos! Just kill me, and may the Emperor forgive you!'

Still the Iron Hands held back, waiting for their quarry to be fully engaged. Kristos moved not a muscle as Captain Stenn was crushed to bloody ruin, the Iron Father's attention held by the target optimisation counters climbing toward one hundred percent in his helmet display. The Raven Guard died one by one, buried in howling foes or melted unto ruin by vomited blasts of green energy.

As the last Raven Guard fell, Kristos sent a single blip of confirmation through his squads' vox-network. Seconds later, the entire breach was awash with flame. Land Raider Redeemers played their firestorm cannons back and forth, bathing the bellowing Orks in white hot fire while bolters thundered and plasma guns howled. Warpboss Zagdakka and his entire retinue were annihilated in a single, perfectly coordinated firestorm.

As the psychic shock of the Weirdboyz' deaths rippled outwards, the Orks howled in sudden, mindless terror or convulsed as their heads exploded like ripe fruit. All across Columnus, the greenskin horde stumbled and stopped, whole swathes dropping dead or running mad as the vast Waaagh! energies broke loose and wreaked havoc. Levelling their weapons, the Imperial forces advanced upon their broken foes, clearing the breach in the fortress walls and taking the fight onto the plains. This time it was the greenskins that were massacred.

Though the war would go on for many weeks yet, with a single blow, Clan Raukaan had won victory for the Imperium. The Orks were ruined as a fighting force, most reduced to dribbling Madboyz and left easy prey for the Imperium's forces. But at the heart of victory lay a gross betrayal, and already voices of dissent were being raised amongst the Iron Fathers. Had bitterness and spite been clad in the raiment of logic? Had the cost of victory been too high? Upon Clan Raukaan's return to Medusa, hard questions would have to be asked...

## CLAN COMPANY DORRVOK (10TH COMPANY)

*As with all other Codex adherent Chapters, the Iron Hands' 10th Company consists of its new recruits, freshly implanted with the Primarch's gene-seed in a ritual known as the Taking of the Soulsteel. The recruits must prove their worth as Scouts before their elevation to full battle-brothers, yet for Iron Hands inductees, this is an especially brutal process. Taught during psycho-indoctrination and dogmatic sermons to revile the weakness of their own flesh, the Scouts of Clan Company Dorrvok must prove themselves capable of acting without weakness under any conditions. They must purge themselves of fear, pain and anger, repressing these feelings with mantras of cold logic, before they will be considered for promotion to the ranks of one of the other clan companies.*

*For the same reason, the initiates find themselves charged with especially dangerous missions. No allowances are made for their relative inexperience, nor their lack of bionics and power armour. Such a violent trial by fire takes its toll and many Scouts do not live to attain the rank of battle-brother, yet those who do are tempered through war into something both less and more than the mere men they once were.*

# THE KRISTOSIAN CONCLAVE

**Following the battle on Columnus, concerns were raised among the Iron Council over the conduct of Iron Father Kristos. Post battle analysis suggested that, while his strategy at Urdri had appeared logical, it smacked of an agenda fulfilled.**

First and foremost was the fact that, while the destruction of the Weirdwaaagh! had hamstrung the Ork forces, Kristos could have had no way of knowing that this would be the case. While the destruction of the Ork threat as a whole might have justified the sacrifice of the Raven Guard force – who, after all, were amongst the Imperium's finest – their deaths were too high a price for simply blunting the momentum of the Ork offensive. Second was the interference with the Raven Guard vox-links, which was confirmed to have originated from an augmetic signal-shroud upon Iron Father Kristos' person. Kristos' supporters, including the respected Iron Captain Graevaar, pointed out that the loss of signal had ensured relations with remaining Raven Guard forces on Columnus were not stretched past breaking point.

## THE IRON COUNCIL

*When it was first convened in the wake of Ferrus Manus' death, the Iron Council chose as their venue a mighty armoured vault deep below the surface of Medusa. The site was large enough to accommodate their number, as well as being exceptionally defensible. The Chapter could not, after all, risk further harm befalling those who would lead it. They have met in this same chamber, known now as the Eye of Medusa, ever since. The Council must always number precisely forty-one Iron Fathers, one for each of the planet's infamous Iron Peaks. Each representative is required to possess sufficient neural augmetics that they can communicate using binary cant and noospheric data-blurts, plugging themselves into their towering iron thrones with spinal plugs and cranial taps. Though this allows huge amounts of debate to take place in a short space of time – not to mention private communications and secret deals beyond counting – all motions and decrees must be read out loud in old Medusan amongst great ceremony and inscribed onto tablets of ironglass in the sight of all. Voting is conducted by delegates dropping ingots into pneumo-tubes in the arms of their thrones. A silver ingot indicates the voting party is in agreement with the motion proposed, while a bronze ingot indicates the opposite. All such votes are anonymous, the ingots falling from shrouded dispensers into their tubes and being swept into the centre of the chamber, where they fall like metal rain onto the device known as the Scales of Logic. Only in such a vote can the Iron Council appoint a single Iron Father as their Chapter's war leader, and then never for more than one year at a time – though the same Iron Father may have his appointment re-ratified in the following year.*

Yet Kristos' detractors on the Council suggested a premeditated intent to ensure the demise of Stenn and his warriors, stemming from an emotional weakness rather than the merciless strength of logic. Finally, there was the most damning evidence of all – Iron Father Kristos had deliberately and wilfully refused inload of information from Shadow Captain Stenn, despite the possibility that this intelligence would have favourably impacted the performance of the Iron Hands. In the face of these allegations, Iron Father Kristos remained unrepentant. He soon drew the support of other Iron Fathers who believed his impeccable record and unquestioning adherence to the doctrines of the Tempering still made Kristos the logical choice for the Chapter's overall war leader. Yet there was sufficient dissent that it seemed only a conclave of the entire Iron Council could resolve the wider issues raised.

With the Chapter's strength spread out across the galaxy, the conclave would not be a simple matter. The Iron Hands could not just abandon their wars lest they appear weak to the rest of the Imperium, or show signs of internal strife. Thus, a rotational series of deployments and campaigns was implemented, the clan companies spreading their strength to confound outside observers and taking it in turns to operate closer to or further from Medusa. Incredibly complex and beautifully conceived, this Chapter-wide system of deployments worked like some vast clockwork engine. In ever-changing combinations, all the Chapter's Iron Fathers were able to attend the Council sessions, which convened three times in each Medusan year. Debates and discussions were worked through methodically and in minute detail, with each matter being advanced to a vote only once all Iron Fathers had been allowed to fully debate its merits.

Though a fair and logical process, it was not a swift one; the years turned to decades as the Kristosian Conclave ground on. What began as an investigation into Kristos' conduct on Columnus soon escalated into the greatest discussion of Chapter philosophy and doctrine since the Tempering. Were certain Iron Fathers more emotionally compromised than they liked to think, and were overt displays of strength and logic being used to veil this weakness? Should all matters be examined from all viewpoints, as seemed only logical? Alternatively, was allowing points of view contradictory to those laid down since time immemorial a flight into whimsy that would compromise the Chapter's strength? Even the true purity of continued technological augmentation was called into question, a matter that quickly became known as the question of the soul. Iron Father Kristos refused to change his stance as the years wound on for, as he claimed, he approached all matters from a position of pure and perfect logic. His supporters – the so-called Kristosians – gained leverage as the debate continued, despite resistance from notable worthies such as Iron Captain Verox, Iron Chaplain Marrus, and the young but gifted Techmarine Kardan Stronos.

All the while the clan companies fought on. As the Kristosian Conclave moved into its second century, Clan Company Raukaan continued to fight with skill and distinction. Now battling under the combined leadership of Iron Chaplain Shulgaar and Epistolary Lydriik, Raukaan exterminated threats to the Emperor's realm wherever they were encountered.

On Baumetricha, Squads Arrvos and Huurek performed a devastating Drop Pod assault against a force of Eldar slave-raiders. Epistolary Lydriik led their crushing offensive, channelling his psychic might through the Mindforge Stave, a storied Chapter relic. During the Xemnoch Schism, Iron Chaplain Shulgaar's Land Raider, *Primarch's Blood*, was at the tip of a Raukaan armoured spearhead that smashed through the Xemnochian lines, but the tank was hit by a macro-cannon shell even as Clan Raukaan stormed onto their objective. Shulgaar climbed from the vehicle's rent hide and, in a bloody battle on the steps of the Shrine to Glory, personally beheaded the apostate Cardinal who had led his people into damnation. Behind him, Raukaan's Techmarines were already restoring *Primarch's Blood* to battle-readiness.

Some years later, fighting at full strength alongside an Adeptus Mechanicus Explorator Fleet, Clan Raukaan performed the efficient and merciless extermination of the mutant tribes of Salem's World. In a systematic campaign of total annihilation that lasted almost a year, the warriors of Clan Raukaan swept every square mile of the planet's surface, defeating seething tides of Chaos worshipping cultists, mutants and freakish Spawn. Their efforts allowed the Explorators to proceed with an undisturbed investigation of the planet's polar ruins, eventually recovering several priceless archeotech artefacts including a fragmented STC. Epistolary Lydriik led the methodical purge of the last mutant cave-stronghold, flanked by four of Raukaan's ancient Dreadnoughts, finally declaring Salem's World secured in the Omnissiah's name just hours before the Explorators completed their own work.

So it went on, with Clan Raukaan adding one ironglass victory plaque after another to their company's Hall of Conquest. There were some who suggested that perhaps Lydriik and Shulgaar displayed a dangerously aggressive style of leadership, on occasion even making decisions that suggested outbursts of emotion rather than logical dictats. These detractors would cite incidents such as Shulgaar's charge at the battle of Naemloch, a vengeful yet illogical offensive that saw him lead over fifty battle-brothers into the teeth of traitor guns. The crashing conflict that followed saw the traitor Space Marines of the Word Bearers hurled back in disarray and their plans on Naemloch brought to ruin. However, the cost in the lives of Raukaan's battle-brothers was significant.

Though none could fault the unyielding fortitude of Shulgaar or his warriors, the accusation remained that the Chaplain had been emotionally compromised when he ordered the attack. For three days Clan Raukaan had held their defences along the Eighty-first Ironline, repelling one Word Bearer assault after another, and looked set to do so until the foe simply ran out of warriors. Yet when the Word Bearers began hurling Ministorum clergymen onto bonfires and broadcasting their screams through massive vox-amps,

Chaplain Shulgaar abandoned his eminently defensible position in favour of an all out-attack, straight into the enemy guns.

Yet for whatever perceived failings their brethren thought they might exhibit, Clan Raukaan's record remained one of successes, albeit bought at what was sometimes seen to be an illogical price.

The Kristosian Conclave reached its two hundredth year in 460.M41 with the Iron Council's lines of division drawn more sharply than ever before. The Chapter was battling on regardless, yet no single Iron Father had been voted as its leader since the conclave began. The Iron Hands direction and focus were beginning to erode as their leaders wrestled with their Chapter's fate, and the Kristosian hard-liners gained ever more influence.

Then came a name, whispered in the darkness of the Chapter's astropathic chambers, that put all other debate to an end. In the Gaudinia System, the presence of the hated Emperor's Children had been reported – operating in great strength, raising cults and subjugating a string of forge and factory worlds. If that were not goad enough, it was said these traitors gave worship to the Sapphire King. Seizing his moment, the now ancient Iron Father Kristos vowed that he would prove the strength of his doctrines and show the purity of his logic in the fires of war. With the assent of the Iron Fathers, and the conclave adjourned, Kristos wasted no time in gathering a mighty force and setting out for the Gaudinia System.

# ARMOURED MIGHT

## ANCIENT FURNOUS

Once an Iron Chaplain within the ranks of Clan Company Raukaan, brother Furnous was mortally wounded amid the catastrophic demise of the traitor Titan *Angron's Fist*. Dragged from the nuclear fires of the Titan's destruction with his flesh burned away or melted to his armour, Furnous' indomitable spirit clung to life long enough for him to be interred within a Dreadnought sarcophagus. To an Iron Hand, there can be few higher honours than elevation to such an overtly mechanical – and thus incalculably strengthened – state, and Furnous has fought to prove himself worthy of this fate for almost four thousand years since. Furnous' assault cannon has claimed thousands of enemy lives, his crushing fist still more. The Venerable Dreadnought's roll of honour tells of victories on Fordecca, Helmgaard, Dawnbreak, Thenoth's World, the Nightmare Spire, the Fireplains and hundreds of others besides. Furnous' seniority among the Dreadnoughts of clan company Raukaan is clear, his wisdom and counsel attended by the company's leaders in all matters of strategy and war. When Raukaan march to battle, Furnous often forms his Dreadnought brethren around him in an unstoppable spearhead, and the former Chaplain bellows canticles of war as he kills, devoting each fallen foe to the Emperor and the Omnissiah alike.

## HEART OF IRON

An especially long-serving transport within Clan Company Raukaan's armoury, *Heart of Iron* is a Rhino APC with an unusually glorious history. The tank first rolled into battle over one thousand years ago, taking to the field against the Ork hordes of Waaagh! Biggfist. During that battle, the *Heart of Iron*'s driver noted that his vehicle possessed an unusually aggressive and dauntless machine spirit. Its engine roared and snarled like an angry beast, and it seemed ever to strain for the front lines. Armed with a pintle storm bolter and a hunter-killer missile, the Rhino fought like a tank twice its size, scything down or ploughing through Orks with impunity and even blowing Warboss Biggfist's personal Battlewagon sky high with a direct hit from its missile. Though the return fire from Biggfist's Nobz blew out *Heart of Iron*'s right-side track unit and crippled the APC's generatorum, the Rhino refused to stay down for long. Even as the Orks swarmed toward *Heart of Iron*, its driver was amazed to see the doughty APC roar back to life, spitting bolt rounds into the aliens' midst and ploughing forward once more to crush the injured Warboss Biggfist himself beneath its damaged tracks. Though battle-scarred, *Heart of Iron* survived its inaugural engagement and fights on today, its hull covered in commendations, honour-badges and commemorative plaques in honour of its achievements.

## MERCILESS

A Hunter anti-aircraft tank that has seen several centuries of service, *Merciless* always lives up to its name. The tank's machine spirit seems almost vindictive in its persecution of the foe – on occasion, its Savant warheads have been seen to seek out and slam into foes even after they have been plucked from the air and dashed to ruin on the ground below. However, *Merciless* is a tireless sentinel: it bears honour-markings from campaigns alongisde Clan Raukaan on Y'Klentis, Raumard and Gorlen's Folly, and is perhaps best known for the tally of xenos slaver craft it reaped during the cleansing of the Hundhar Clustar.

## GORGON'S FURY

A Predator in Ghaarvan Squadron, *Gorgon's Fury* rolled off the forge-lines on Mars little more than a century ago. However, the tank has already earned a reputation as a monster hunter, employing its autocannon to deadly effect in numerous battles against the Tyranids of Hive Fleet Leviathan. On Jouraga, *Gorgon's Fury* led a column of twenty battle tanks which were deployed to bring down the massive Tyranid bio-horrors that were rampaging through the Prime Laborium, a task that they set to with a will.

Looming, armoured beasts were torn apart, crashing to the ground with acidic blood gushing from gaping wounds. Subterranean monsters exploded from the highway only to be raked with fire. Then came the bio-titan. *Gorgon's Fury* struck – calmly lining up his shots, the gunner allowed his tank's machine spirit to guide his aim to the cracked armour around the bio-titan's neck, and blew its head off in a shower of gore. The creature was killed clean, its death commemorated by a unique honour badge inscribed on *Gorgon's Fury's* hull.

# THE GAUDINIAN HERESY

The Iron Hands fleet that translated into the Gaudinia System was huge. Iron Father Kristos had assumed the mantle of war leader and had assembled more than eight hundred Iron Hands under his control. This was the greatest deployment of the Chapter for centuries, and was accompanied by the majority of the Iron Council. The Kristosians were present in force, yet Stronos, Verox and Marrus were among a number of Iron Father Kristos' detractors also on board the ships of the fleet.

Initial auguries showed that all six worlds of the Gaudinia System were overrun by mutants and heretics, yet according to the Astropathic distress call, the Emperor's Children had only been seen around the factory world of Gaudinia Prime. This, then, would be the Iron Hands' primary objective. While smaller strike forces peeled off to begin the systematic purge of the other worlds, a core of three hundred Iron Hands – including Clan Companies Raukaan and Sorrgol in their entirety – made straight for Gaudinia Prime and approached high orbit. Here they were to face their first signs of opposition as they were forced to blast their way through a scattered cordon of warped turncoat warships.

The craft had once been system monitors, Imperial Navy frigates whose crew had turned to the worship of the Sapphire King. These craft now showed signs of their debasement, weird clashing colours and vestigial mutant outgrowths carpeting their hulls. Thankfully though, the foe was few in number and came on in a disorganised rush as though racing one another willingly to their deaths. With calm efficiency, the Iron Hands ships drew up line abreast, maximised their torpedo and lance spreads, and blasted the traitor ships into atoms. Not a single enemy craft reached battery range, each flaring and dying as their Warp coils overloaded and their hulls broke apart. Ploughing forward through the drifting wreckage that remained, the Iron Hands made orbit with mechanical precision, releasing swarms of space-capable servo-skulls to scan for further foes.

As the auto-divination shrines chattered out reams of parchment, the Iron Fathers puzzled over the readings from the planet below. Gaudinia Prime was a factory world, its entire landmass given over to the processing of raw materials and the manufacture of weapons for use by the Imperial Guard. It was registered as possessing a labour population of approximately 362 billion souls, spread out across the huge planet's surface. Now, however, the world's biomass appeared both to exceed that sum and, impossibly, to be less than zero, the figure fluctuating madly even as the scans came in. Stranger still, from the oceanic algae farms of the coasts to the mountaintop spaceports and their cargo-thrall townships, there was no sign of any life whatsoever, and no trace of the Emperor's Children. Instead, all signs of life now appeared to be concentrated in one small map-segment of the primary manufactorum, a nation-sized industrial sprawl in the planet's southern hemisphere. Iron Fathers Stronos and Verrox counselled caution – the twisted machinations of Chaos were impossible to predict, and logic

dictated that they gather further data before launching their attack. Iron Father Kristos was inflexible as ever, driven by his determination to destroy any surviving Emperor's Children forces before they could escape. Hesitation was for the weak, he announced, before ordering a drop assault in full force upon the primary manufactorum. Throughout the fleet, Iron Hands disconnected from simulus chambers and apothecarian augmentation-frames, submitted to the attentions of the arming servitors and marched to their Stormravens, Thunderhawks and Drop Pods. The Iron Hands would follow the trail of freakish lifesigns to the foe they sought, and there would crush them utterly.

The Iron Hands descended in fire and fury, their Drop Pods and landing craft turning the skies dark with their contrails. Holding to doctrines that had served them well since the days of the Great Crusade, the entire force mustered their strength in a single, mile-wide drop zone to the south-west of the central processing hub. Drop Pods crashed through roofs and smashed craters into ferrocrete roadways, squads of black-clad Space Marines surging forth and spreading out to secure their landing sites, and Raukaan's massed Dreadnoughts marched forward in force. Behind them, heavier landers descended to deploy squadrons of rumbling tanks and Centurions into the statue-lined squares and thoroughfares of the manufactorum. Squads of Bikes and Land Speeders, the preferred steeds of Clan Morlaag, raced out along labour-processionals and over generatorum sprawls in search of contacts, while Scouts of Clan Dorrvok crept across rooftops and filtered down into the sewer systems to hunt for threats. No sign of any foe could be seen.

The streets of the Primary Manufactorum were empty, save for wind-blown litter. Shrines to the Omnissiah stood empty, their neglected electrocandles burned out. Curdled broth dripped from feeder-tubes in the nutritionals and formed puddles whose skins of mould attested to many days of disuse. Everywhere the Iron Hands kicked down doors or smashed through walls, habs, workshops and medicae stations stood empty under a dusty film of abandonment. Still, the Iron Hands' auspexes were reading jittering life-signs from all around. As they worked their way toward the central processing hub they began to hear sounds of industry. Bolters swung up and squads moved into battle formations as the Space Marines approached the vast iron dome of the hub, listening to the frantic cacophony that rang from within.

The hub stood almost two thousand feet high at its crest, ten miles across at its base, and appeared to be sealed tight as though against attack or unnaturally severe weather. From within came a maddened din of machinery interspersed with hissing groans and wheezing screams that caused even the taciturn sons of Ferrus Manus to look askance at one another. Borne on the wind was a stench like burning flesh mixed with some kind of bilious sweetness as though gallons of perfume had been spilled into rotted faeces. Impassive, Iron Father Kristos ordered entrances to be made in the dome's walls. He and the other Iron Fathers would lead the warriors of Clan Raukaan to discover what manner of devilry lurked within.

Ironclad Dreadnoughts and Assault Centurions moved in, swiftly tearing yawning breaches through which the warriors of Clan Raukaan followed. The tight confines of the processing hub forced the clan company's tanks and Thunderfire Cannons to remain behind with the rest of the host to hold the vast plaza that ringed the dome. Refusing to show concern, the battle-brothers pressed forward regardless. However, within moments the advance faltered as the Space Marines were confronted by the hellish interior of the dome. Once, the central processing hub had been a hive of gantries, conveyor belts, towering machines and labouring work-gangs. Now it was a vision of hell, for the workers and machines had become one.

## ENGINES OF THE DAMNED

Billions of Imperial citizens had been crammed into this ten-mile space, their flesh and bones melded with the steel, circuits and pipes of the machines. Pistons rose and fell with manic speed, driven by great tangles of bulging human limbs. Melted masses of flesh formed twisted gantries where faces writhed and moaned. Human torsos, skin seared and impossibly bloated, jutted from boiler-stacks. They shrieked endlessly as steaming blood vented from their eyes. Here, cogs of bone and raw, bloodied nerves rotated at breakneck speed. There, daemonic weapons were thrust along fleshy conveyor belts by the peristaltic motion of a billion disembodied tongues. Worst of all was the din, a discordant industrial thunder of jarring voices that tore at the air until the Iron Hands were forced to dampen their audio-receptors.

Clan Raukaan advanced into this nauseating bedlam, weapons raised and anger boiling beneath their self-control. The insult was obvious, for here was steel and flesh combined to create something greater than either. Warped weaponry churned through the pulsating machines at breakneck speed, its construction abhorrent yet undeniably perfect. These flesh engines were monstrous beyond words, a daemonic perversion that undermined everything they held dear. Centuries of training and subconscious conditioning fought to suppress the revulsion they felt as they pressed forward. The squads voxed back and forth, Clan Raukaan's Tactical and Assault Squads taking the lead while the Dreadnoughts, Devastators and Centurions watched their flanks.

They had advanced almost to the heart of the structure, their armour stained with steaming gore and trickling fluids, when the compulsions struck. Assault Squad Neim were stalking along a walkway of writhing wires and muscle, Iron Fathers Kristos and Graevaar in their midst. Suddenly Kristos

stumbled to a stop, his whirring limbs stuttering as he missed a step. Graevaar cocked his head quizzically, flexing his powerfist and scanning the machines around him. There was frantic movement everywhere but nothing to indicate the reason for the Iron Father's sudden hesitation. Kristos gazed around in a daze, sweeping his augmetic eyes across the flesh machines and muttering.

'Can you not see it, Graevaar? Do you not hear its song? The perfect utility... the efficiency... the strength...' Suddenly, before anyone could react, Iron Father Kristos plunged a nest of his mechadendrites into the fleshwet receptors of the machines around him. Graevaar's living eye widened and Squad Neim raised their weapons in shock as Kristos convulsed, jaws stretching wide to emit a strangled whine of scrapcode. The sound rose in volume, Kristos' voice seeming to multiply into a shrieking binary chorus that swelled by the second. Iron Captain Graevaar broke his paralysis, lunging forward to disconnect the convulsing Kristos, but it was already far too late. The ancient Iron Father's mechadendrites bulged obscenely, fleshy matter squirting from between their segmented links, and Kristos howled with a thousand voices as his body began to warp and twist.

What living flesh remained to him swelled rapidly, writhing and bulging as it grew. Clumps of snaking, blood-slick wires and tubes burst from between armour segments, coiling around his vein-stretched limbs as they elongated obscenely. The Iron Father's servo-harness melded with his grossly swollen skin, its limbs becoming monstrous, insectile things that ended in slavering mouths and chitinous claws. Threat runes lit up across Squad Neim's visors as the seething horror that had once been Iron Father Kristos tore free of the flesh engines and surged forward. The machine-spawn emitted an ululating howl, bladed limbs lashing out to scythe through Graevaar's waist and tear him in two amid sheets of blood and sparks. The horror ploughed on into Squad Neim, Kristos' tortured body convulsing as he tore apart his former brothers. Even as the Assault Squad belatedly opened fire, the story was repeating throughout the dome.

Everywhere, Kristosian Iron Fathers were being overcome by the twisted perfection of the flesh engines – the harder they attempted to repress their urges with logic, the faster they succumbed. The effect was already spreading to the most heavily augmetic members of Clan Raukaan. Dozens of battle-brothers lunged helplessly for the hellish machines, many gunned down by their horrified brethren as their weakness revealed itself. The rest jammed augmetics into the fleshy flanks of the machines, cramming foetid tubes into their eyes and mouths as they surrendered to the scrap-code's siren song. Even as the machine-spawn bloated and twisted, turning upon their revolted squad-mates, reality began to shudder and buckle.

The temperature soared and plunged as a static-laden whine filled the air. Epistolary Lydriik yelled a warning as howling daemonic rents tore into being, shimmering portals of pearlescent smoke that yawned wider with every moment. From each rent flowed perfumed streamers of ectoplasmic vapour that clung and slithered like liquid flesh. From amid these vile fronds burst squealing, gasping masses of Daemons, rippling silks and glimmering jewels set amongst jagged bone claws and lashing, leathery tongues.

With them came warriors of the Emperor's Children, their gaudily daubed armour and thrumming weapons jarring with the howling, swirling beings that surrounded them.

Madness engulfed the dome. Bolters and flamers roared, yet Clan Raukaan were all but buried in foes. Machine-spawn reeled drunkenly through volleys of fire, smashing battle-brothers off their feet with every blow as capering Daemons fell upon them with shrieks of glee. Whiplash talons and glistening blades hacked at flesh and steel amid peals of laughter. As more Iron Hands clamped down upon their suppressed horror and rage, so did more burst into mutation, their locked-down emotions haemorrhaging and rupturing under the Sapphire King's influence.

Amid roiling clouds of poisoned perfume, the bejewelled Daemon itself strode from a gaping portal to bask in the demise of the Chapter it had brought to ruin. Tall and lithe, with great claws and silken flesh, the Sapphire King revelled in the death that surrounded it, shrieking praise to its god for its inevitable victory. Yet as Kardan Stronos watched another brother of Squad Riis degenerate before his eyes, revelation struck like a thunderbolt. He was disgusted by these abominations, furious at the weakness of the brothers who had allowed themselves to fall. Crushing those feelings would not undo them, only cause them to curdle into corruption, and therein lay the snare. Strength lay not in cutting himself off from his emotions, but from shackling them to his iron will. With a roar of effort, Stronos harnessed the roiling emotions that threatened to tear him apart, blasting shots into the mutating battle-brother before him as he vented his disgust. Activating his vox, Stronos barked commands to the forces around him.

## A DEADLY PATH

*It was at the precise moment that Ferrus Manus' head was scythed from his shoulders by the traitor Fulgrim that the Sapphire King came into being. Spawned from the psychic bow wave of Manus' death, this Daemon was forged from the Primarch's frustrated pride, his boiling anger and sorrow, and from his shame. From the moment of its birth, the Sapphire King fed on the repressed emotions of the soul-scarred Iron Hands. It basked in their chained desperation, bound to their fate by the emotions they felt but would not express. The Daemon bedevilled them across the centuries, offering opportunities for damnation disguised as steps away from the weakness they so feared. It nudged the minds of Imperial officials and potential foes, forever seeking to goad the Iron Hands into spending away their humanity like coin. The Chapter bent their every effort to purging the weaknesses of the flesh, never realising that the more they demonised their wants and needs, the greater the hold the spectre of their repressed emotions gained upon them.*

*As the Kristosian Conclave reached its zenith, the Sapphire King judged the Iron Hands ripe to fall and set its trap in motion. Each Iron Hand carried within his heart a rancid seed, a bomb of repressed passions that could erupt to destroy him at any moment. The Daemon would simply provide the spark to light the flame and watch the Chapter burn upon a pyre of their own emotions.*

'Release your anger brothers, let it out before the foe destroys you with it!' Slowly at first, then faster in a spreading wave, the battle-brothers began to disengage their inhibitor protocols and loose furious battle cries. Emotional floodgates burst open and the Sapphire King shrieked its rage as the repressed energies that had fuelled its spell were vented like steam from a boiler.

Freed from the debilitating Warp-craft, the surviving warriors of Clan Raukaan gave vent to their revulsion, blasting the Daemons apart in rains of ectoplasmic filth or tearing them limb from shimmering limb. Stronos began a coordinated retreat from the dome, the depleted clan company falling back by squad, fighting furiously all the way. They drew Warpspawn and traitors alike into overlapping fields of fire and tore them apart in their hundreds. Dreadnoughts performed sudden counter-charges that pushed the foe back, their massive fists pulping Daemons into paste while their guns roared. Fighting their way free with uncharacteristic ferocity, the Iron Hands broke out into the windswept plaza before the dome, the foe still howling and shrieking at their heels.

The moment the last battle-brother backed through the breach, the tanks of Clans Raukaan struck. Smashing into the flanks of the horde as it flooded forth, their thundering fire and grinding tracks exterminated the Daemons in droves. Still the otherworldly horrors came on, the Sapphire King striding amid a cadre of Noise Marines. The Daemon towered over its followers like a heathen idol given life. Centurions of Squad Haarkol stormed toward the beast, their weapons blazing, but were driven back by the howling guns of the Emperor's Children with ears and eyes bleeding until their helmets swilled with blood. The Sapphire King berated the Iron Hands in a clashing voice both beautiful and grating – had it not granted them a marvellous gift? Had it not given them the chance to embrace a strength like nothing they had ever felt, to shed mortal weakness forever? Yet they – ignorant droning machine-men that they were – had proven themselves as dull as rusted iron, and undeserving of its blessings. Now they would all die.

Daemonettes on whirling, bladed chariots ploughed through the melee, lopping off heads and limbs as they passed. Machine-spawn drove pulsating tentacles of nerve-cable into the hulls of tanks and Dreadnoughts, the vehicles shuddering and bulging with vile corruption as their crews drowned in fleshy foulness. The warping screams of the Sapphire King and its underlings shattered armour, reduced bionics to sparking ruin, and caused eyes and organs to rupture in showers of blood. The remaining warriors of Clan Raukaan desparately struggled to hold their lines in the face of such a disorienting attack, and it seemed like they still might lose the battle.

Then, with an impassioned roar that rang over the battle, Epistolary Lydriik charged. With him ran his command squad, bionic limbs pumping and bolters blazing. The Librarian swept the Mindforge Stave in great arcs, each whistling blow hammering traitors from their feet and blowing them apart with thrumming blasts of psychic force. First one Noise Marine, then another, was sent sailing through the air, mashed armour leaking gore as they died. Around him, Lydriik's warriors fought with a fury they had never before allowed themselves to display, piston-limbed blows lent a sledgehammer strength that staved in plumed helms and hacked through gaudy breastplates.

With a supersonic squeal of outrage, the towering Daemon lashed out, coral-hued claws snipping the arm from Apothecary Ruumas and punching through the faceplate of Brother Lorrgus. Lydriik narrowed his eyes as the beast towered over him, forging his hate and anger into a single white-hot star behind his eyes. Even as the Sapphire King swept its talons down towards him, the Librarian unleashed his roiling powers, sending them surging from the tip of the Mindforge Stave and straight into the freakish Daemon's face. Tainted blood splattered out amid a spinning shrapnel cloud of warped black bone and flickering jewels. Decapitated by the thunderous blast, the Sapphire King's body reared backward, claws flailing, rancid black filth jetting violently from its stump of a neck. Still standing, the Daemon's form convulsed, bulged obscenely, and then exploded in a spray of noisome black filth that stank like rotted perfume.

Their lord destroyed, the Daemons of Slaanesh began to flicker and fade, their strength deserting them by the second until they faded away like smoke on the breeze. Impossibly outnumbered, the last few Emperor's Children fought on with mad glee, but in the face of Clan Raukaan's wrath they were swiftly blasted into bloodied ruin.

The surviving machine-spawn had died with the Sapphire King, their revolting bodies haemorrhaging black sludge and perfumed foulness. As the dust settled around the last fallen corpse, Clan Raukaan were left with just the howling wind, the muted, horrified murmurs of the surviving battle-brothers, and the distant clamour of the flesh-engines pounding ever onward. Iron Chaplain Shulgaar surveyed the battlefield that had come so close to damning his Chapter forever and knew what must be done.

'Return to the ships,' he ordered, his voice a grating mechanical snarl. 'From orbit we will burn it all. Nothing remains for us here.'

# A NEW RESOLVE

**On Gaudinia Prime, the Iron Hands had survived a deadly trap, yet it had taken its toll. Lost manpower could be recouped over time, lost vehicles repaired or replaced, yet the psychological wounds the Chapter had suffered might yet prove fatal.**

Nearly a third of the Iron Council had fallen into the Daemon's trap and been lost to corruption, along with many of their battle-brothers. Should this revelation ever reach the Inquisition, it would be disastrous. The Iron Hands found themselves forced to question the very principles upon which they based their existence. The Kristosians had held absolutely to the tenets of the Tempering, their literal interpretation but an expression of the direction in which the Chapter had been moving for thousands of years. Iron over flesh; logic over emotion; the merciless, relentless purge of those weaknesses that threatened ruin. Yet what if this very obsession with emotional excision and the perfection of the machine was a weakness in its own right?

Much reduced, reeling in the wake of the revelations they had been forced to confront, the Iron Council threatened to disintegrate. In an emergency session of the council, panic bubbled beneath the surface as dozens of theories, arguments and proposals were aired and dismissed. How could the Chapter continue, voices asked, if everything they did, everything they stood for, was tainted by the very weakness they had striven against for so long?

It was in this moment that Kardan Stronos came to the fore. Rising from his throne, Stronos unplugged himself and addressed his brothers with his unalloyed, natural voice. The Chapter had been given a gift, he announced. Though their foes tried to lay them low and corrupt their purpose, the Iron Hands had instead seen the potential for darkness within themselves, and had overcome it.

> 'Our Chapter was driven to the very lip of the precipice. We were forced to stare over its edge into the stygian depths, into the darkness that awaits us should ever we fall. Yet fall we did not! What saved us from this terrible plunge, brothers? What has proved our redemption? Not logic. Not the desperate, dogmatic purge of all things perceived as weak. It was our souls that saved us, and the strength we hold within ourselves. Our courage. Our choler. It was the qualities which make us more than just unthinking steel that pulled us back from the brink.'
>
> *- Kardan Stronos, address to the Eye of Medusa*

It was at the booming culmination of this speech that he delivered his immortal words, a quote that would be enshrined upon Ironglass plaques across Medusa and beyond from that day forth.

'With steel we are stronger, but without a soul we are nothing.' This would be the first day in ten thousand years that the Eye of Medusa had rung to the sound of applause. Despite disquiet from the few remaining Kristosians and the Voice of Mars, Kardan Stronos was elected war leader that same day, and has been reelected at every opportunity since.

The words of Kardan Stronos had not affected an instantaneous change in the Iron Hands. One speech could not reverse thousands of years of indoctrination, even had every last Iron Hand been open to its message. Yet it was the beginning of something – a slow but palpable shift in attitude that would take centuries, beginning with the Iron Council and filtering outward as the years rolled by. Following Epistolary Lydriik and Iron Chaplain Shulgaar's elevation as Iron Fathers, the number of Librarians and Iron Chaplains accorded this honour steadily grew. Logic still drove the Iron Council's calculations, yet they were always on guard against the dangers of heresy, and efforts were made to curb the most inhuman of their impulses. Most importantly, on the battlefield, the Iron Hands tempered mechanical logic with an edge of their Primarch's wrath. They would never reject the steel in their hearts, yet many battle-brothers now forged it anew in the fires of their rekindled souls.

## RAUKAAN ASCENDANT

The warriors of Clan Company Raukaan took well to the teachings of Kardan Stronos. Their Iron Chaplains tended their brothers' souls, striving to steer them from the paths of complete emotional disconnect or obsessive self-mechanisation. Use of the simulus chambers was reduced until some clan companies – Raukaan amongst them – barely used them at all. Face-to-face briefings were now preferred, alongside the tactical flexibility of acting without pre-set parameters.

The Chapter still looked down upon those who chose passion or wrath over cold, hard logic. Yet they now recognised that true strength came not from fleeing their emotions, or attempting to amputate them altogether, but from achieving mastery over them. As Iron Father Feirros would often tell new Techmarines upon their return from Mars, a Titan is a mighty weapon of the Omnissiah, but without the fires of its reactor it is but cold, dead metal.

As the years passed, there were still those amongst the Iron Council who viewed Stronos' methods with suspicion, or even outright alarm. Some warned that he was walking the same path as did the Primarch ten thousand years ago, and that he was leading his Chapter not away from weakness but towards it. Yet even these die-hard malcontents could not deny the Chapter's many victories in the centuries that followed, nor that Clan Company Raukaan led the charge.

Raukaan, their notoriously aggressive temperament fusing well with Stronos' doctrines, distinguished themselves in one battle after another. On Ultrense IV, they were deployed to repel a Tyranid splinter fleet that surged from the Gynomarr Cluster. At the final battle in the Sanctum of Defiance, the entire clan company deployed in a single chain of unbreakable steel, tanks and infantry drawn up side by side to exterminate the last, overwhelming charge of the Tyranids. Their guns roared with mechanical fury as beasts beyond counting poured in a tide through the Sanctum's great arch. Casings and spent power-packs piled in drifts around power-armoured legs. Machine spirit fire-fields and helmet augurs overlapped with seamless efficiency, missiles and shells and bolts pouring like rain into the avalanche of flesh. Still the Tyranids pressed forward, showers of bio-acid and whining bone projectiles smashing battle-brothers from their feet or chewing through the armour of mighty tanks. Yard by desperate yard the Tyranids came, scrambling over growing mountains of their own dead, yet they could not reach their foes. The final Tyranid organism, a monster the size of a Baneblade, shuddered and crashed down dead mere inches from Clan Raukaan's battle line.

Elsewhere, their conquests were no less inspiring. The Drakonmarch System was cleansed of Orks in a merciless series of lightning offensives, Clan Raukaan crushing each tribe of greenskins before they could gather their vastly superior numbers. On Haedese, Iron Chaplain Shulgaar and Iron Captain Grolvoch faced the towering Daemon Prince Magnathrax, cutting the unnatural monster down even as its cult was exterminated by spearhead thrusts of Predators, Vindicators and Land Raiders. When the brutish Warboss Krugg led a mighty horde of his Blood Axe Boyz in an attack upon Noctule's Hope, a handful of warriors from Clan Raukaan stood behind the now Chief Librarian Lydriik in defence of the famed Healer's Spire. Battle erupted amongst the medicae shrines of that holy city, the Orks pouring through the streets in ramshackle columns of tanks. Yet Lydriik led one perfectly executed ambush after

another, carefully preserving his warriors and the three Dreadnoughts that accompanied them through days then weeks of conflict. Krugg himself led a final, sledgehammer offensive intended to exterminate Lydriik' force, but was instead messily slain when the long awaited reinforcements from Clans Avernii and Sorrgol descended in wrath.

## THE FALL OF BROMOCH
Never was the successful fusion of iron and flesh more evident than when Clan Company Raukaan was deployed to the war-torn world of Bromoch. A hive world that had once boasted vast oceans teeming with life, Bromoch had been torn asunder when a vast mechanised tomb complex awoke beneath its surface. Yawning fissures broke open in the deepest oceanic trenches, trillions of gallons of water draining away in a matter of days to leave a stinking quagmire of saltmud and rotting biomatter that covered half the world. From this awful wasteland rose legions of mechanised warriors, their armour thick with verdigris and muck. It would be over a century before the Imperium officially recognised and put a name to these terrible beings, yet the governor of Bromoch did not need an official designation to recognise the risen warriors for the terrible threat they were. They marched upon the hive cities in ranks many hundreds of thousands strong, eldritch engines of war hovering above them as they came. The outmatched Planetary Defence Force levies rushed to man their posts, and a frantic call for help was sent.

Only weeks later, the ships of Clan Company Raukaan made orbit over Bromoch, accompanied by Kardan Stronos himself. Lydriik and Shulgaar still led the clan company, their command now shared with the adamantium-skulled Iron Captain Grolvoch and an eccentric Master of the Forge by the name of Feirros, whose gallows humour was notorious throughout the Chapter. As these five inspected a holomap of Bromoch on the bridge of the Strike Cruiser *Solemn Silence*, it became clear that the planet was already lost. The PDF regiments had fought bravely, but they were outnumbered and hopelessly outclassed by their deathless foes. One hive city after another had fallen, their streets swarming with metallic horrors, until only the Hive Primus remained. There the defenders still held out against impossible odds, fighting tooth and nail to hold their barricades while bulk lifters and cargo barques fled into orbit bearing thousands upon thousands of refugees.

Once, the Iron Hands might have dismissed the people of Bromoch as weak and unworthy of their aid, but no more. Yet they were not Space Wolves or Black Templars, to rush headlong into the breach at Hive Primus and save all they could. Instead, Tactical Squad Taloch were despatched in a Stormraven Gunship, accompanied by Iron Chaplain Shulgaar – they would assist the evacuation, applying their fearsome presence and infinitely superior grasp of logistics to ensure matters proceeded apace. Meanwhile, the rest of Clan Raukaan prepared for an immediate combat drop. Telltale energy signatures had been detected emanating from one of the great oceanic rifts, signatures that matched those given off by the machines seized centuries earlier on Dawnbreak. The Iron Hands did not recognise these monstrous mechanical aliens, yet they knew their works. This time, however, Kardan Stronos led Raukaan not to claim the engines of the past but to destroy them.

The great trench ran almost eighty miles end to end, gaping over one hundred metres wide and surrounded by hard-baked mud and teetering, desiccated drifts of what had once been thriving coral. From its depths leaked a leprous green glow, and it was into this shimmering corona that the warriors of Clan Raukaan plunged. Drop Pods hurtled down in a tight knot, whistling between the jaws of the chasm and plummeting ever deeper on trails of flame.

As the transports fell, the glow around them turned to a lurid glare, and then they were falling into a vast cavern. A good three thousand feet below the planet's crust, the cave was cyclopean in scale, dominated by immense ziggurats of glassy black stone that swarmed with robotic alien workers and warriors. The Drop Pods crashed down in a tight grouping between these mighty edifices, Iron Hands and Dreadnoughts bursting free to engage the foe that surrounded them.

Stronos led the charge at the head of Squad Kuurvan, his bolter kicking in his fist and the Axe of Medusa cleaving through metallic bodies with every swing. A trio of Dreadnoughts – Venerable Furnous and two Ironclads – began to carve a path through the milling automata. Weapons roared and mighty fists crushed the metal-skinned xenos to twisted wreckage. The strange, deathless creatures were reacting now, slowly but surely bringing waves of floating metal constructs to bear against the invading Iron Hands, and Clan Raukaan's Techmarines stalked in the Dreadnoughts' wake, ready to tend to their ancient charges should they fall to enemy fire.

Suddenly, the foes ranks were torn by fresh blasts as a wing of Stormraven Gunships roared overhead, flanking the mighty form of the Thunderhawk *Forgestar*. The aircraft dropped low, their thrusters roaring as their ramps yawned open to disgorge Thunderfire Cannons and a wave of Centurions into the fight. The vox rang with Master Feirros' grim laughter as he led them forth. Though the foe's numbers were vast, most of their leaders were far above, coordinating the final battle against Hive Primus – soulless machines, they could not compete with the vital, crushing force of Clan Raukaan's offensive.

Finally, at the base of the largest ziggurat, Feirros summoned a pair of lumpen servitors bearing a heavy iron chest covered in panels and dials. As the device was slammed down into the dirt, Feirros busied himself with its activation while the warriors of Clan Raukaan formed an impenetrable wall around him. Here and there, blasts of green energy flayed the armour and flesh from a battle-brother or blew a vehicle apart in a roiling ball of flame, yet the automatons could not break through. All the while, Kardan Stronos remained vox-linked to Iron Captain Grolvoch, ignoring his subconscious protocols as they balked at the rising casualty rate. Clan Raukaan's guns thundered a merciless staccato, punctuated by the howling blasts of lascannons and plasma guns as they built ramparts of mangled mechanical bodies all around their position.

Finally, Iron Captain Grolvoch voxed through – the chance of recovering further refugees from Hive Primus now stood at less than 20 percent; the Iron Hands' agreed cut-off point. With a curt command, Stronos ordered Clan Raukaan's

aircraft down, Iron Father Lydriik directing furious covering fire from the Devastator Squads as the battle-brothers scrambled back aboard their craft. Ramjets roared and the Stormraven Gunships hurtled skyward, *Forgestar* covering their retreat with a thunderous bombardment of fire. In their wake they left the iron chest, cascades of glowing runes flickering across its surface and its energy shielding soaking up a rain of green fire as its timer counted down to zero.

Even as the airborne Clan Raukaan burst from the rift and into the open sky, their ancient ordnance detonated. Servo-bonded chains of crystalline prisms shattered, releasing howling swarms of insane machine spirits bent only on destruction. The spirits flowed outward in a tide, corroding and devouring every mechanical system in their path. Nothing was safe, the bodies and weapons of the xenos burned along with the weapons and systems of those few defenders who remained. Behind them – as the various craft of the Iron Hands pushed hard for the upper atmosphere and their waiting cruisers – Bromoch plunged helplessly into a new dark age, the planet's orbital silos detonating spontaneously and filling the skies with drifting, radioactive clouds. In orbit, a ragged flotilla of refugee ships gathered to watch the planet die. The Iron Hands, inscrutable as ever, denied the existence of any mechanical foe in the wake of the disaster, carefully discrediting those wild tales told by the refugees. Though the Chapter might still keep their secrets, millions of Imperial lives had been saved thanks to the strength and determination of Clan Company Raukaan.

## AN UNCERTAIN FUTURE

Though at times they may have embraced Stronos' way to a lesser extent, the ongoing battles of the other clan companies were no less heroic. The efforts of the Chapter bolstered key war zones and led Imperial Crusades to victory. While the Iron Hands were still viewed with suspicion by much of the Imperium, they were also respected for their unbending strength.

Yet still the galaxy has darkened around the Iron Hands, disdainful of whatever personal victories they may have achieved. The Iron Council has seen long-standing allies fall to madness or corruption, and thought back with disquiet to days long passed. They have looked on as great swathes of the Imperium have been plunged into darkness, and brooded upon what the future may bring. They have viewed the changes even within their own Chapter, changes wrought by Kardan Stronos and epitomised by the resurgent Clan Raukaan, and drawn parallels with a bitterly mourned father and his final, awful fate.

With so many threats to face, with sanity and surety eroding all around them, the logic of the Calculum Rationale no longer appears enough. Finally, the Iron Council have declared another great conclave. This gathering, the Grand Calculation, will be used to determine the future of the entire Iron Hands Chapter.

# THE GRAND CALCULATION

**A war engulfs the Imperium now, greater than any it has faced before. As they always have, the Iron Council believe first and foremost in the overwhelming application of force, and they cannot simply scatter their Chapter's strength into the fire.**

The Iron Hands will not trust in the vagaries of fate to direct where they should stand during Mankind's final battle. Instead, the Iron Council will consider every factor, assess every threat, and determine where their warriors will serve the greatest purpose. Their successor Chapters, too, will be considered in this equation – envoys already wing their way through the Warp to secure common cause with the Brazen Claws, the Iron Lords, even the Sons of Medusa. While the Iron Council's debate grinds on, Stronos and a handful of his closest supporters continue to direct the Chapter in war, battling to hold back the darkness while the Iron Council's Grand Calculation is completed.

A veritable conclave of Iron Fathers leads Clan Raukaan in these dark days – Chief Librarian Lydriik, grim-faced Chaplain Shulgaar, Iron Captain Grolvoch and eccentric old Master of the Forge Feirros. These four have been the masters of Clan Company Raukaan for several hundred years, and have filled these centuries with glorious victory over the foes of Man. It is their private belief, based upon a mixture of cogitation and gut instinct, that the Chapter will choose one of a select few foes against which to level its might. Yet even they cannot predict where their Chapter will strike, or whether it will elect to do so in time.

As Hive Fleet Leviathan inveigles its tentacles ever further into the galaxy, the Tyranid race reveals ever more of its abhorrent nature. A single great and terrible machine, forged entirely from corrupt alien flesh, seeking only to consume the Emperor's realm as fuel for its own blasphemous existence – not only do the hive fleets represent an incalculable threat to the survival of Mankind, but in the eyes of the Iron Hands, they are a dire abomination. Indeed, Kardan Stronos himself has been despatched to face this very threat, lending his strength and wisdom to the fight against Leviathan.

With their strength increasing daily as more and more tomb worlds awaken, the dynasties of the Necrons present an ever greater threat. If the Tyranids offend the Iron Hands with their revolting biomechanical nature, the Necrons are more blasphemous yet. In the eyes of the Omnissiah, such soulless machine-men are the ultimate expression of heresy – within the ranks of Clan Raukaan, there are many who would gladly spend their lives to see this scourge destroyed.

Yet a third course presents itself, a more shadowed purpose guessed at through assembled hints and portents. Twelve times has this foe struck at the Imperium, each time leaving a trail of clues to his ultimate intentions. Twelve times the actions of Abaddon the Despoiler have been faultlessly catalogued by the Iron Hands, their every possible ramification extrapolated by conclaves of Iron Fathers performing logic-spirit seances. Over the centuries, the Iron Hands have become ever more certain of this

foe's intentions, even gathering sufficient information to hypothesise the very hour at which the Despoiler may strike his final blow. Many amongst the Iron Council now argue that this, surely, is where their Chapter must deploy its might, for no war could be more vital. Yet, insular as they are, the Iron Hands have not seen fit to share their calculations with the wider Imperium – were their conclusions to prove incorrect, the Iron Hands would be made to look foolish and frightened to their allies. This is something the Iron Council will never risk, so their warning remains ungiven as their debate grinds ever on.

Should a conclusion be drawn, should the successor Chapters join with their founders once more, should support be offered by the Voice of Mars – thus far noticeably silent in the conclave – then a mighty weapon indeed would be forged. Where this hammerblow would fall, against which threat to Humanity, none can say, yet its impact would be devastating indeed. Upon that day, Clan Company Raukaan would march to war alongside a gathering of their brothers like nothing seen since the days of the Great Crusade. However, the Iron Council's deliberations run long, with no end in sight, and every day the end draws a little closer. Clan Company Raukaan fight on beside their brothers, every battle they win another step along the road to redemption. Yet they can only hope, as the fires rise around them, that it will not all be in vain.

## THE FORGECHAIN

*While the Iron Hands use skull-studs to denote long service in the same manner as other Chapters, in recent years greater value has been placed upon the strange augmetic known as the Forgechain. Taking the form of a series of augmetic vertebrae, each linked to next by complex strands of neural relays, the Forgechain quite literally puts steel in each battle-brother's spine. Each new vertebrae torn loose and replaced represents the Iron Hand's acceptance into another clan company. Each company forge their own links from their own chosen materials, the better to reinforce the recipient's new allegiance. Dorrvok, for example, use unadorned steel to form the first vertebrae for each of their newly blooded Scouts. Clan Sorrgol's vertebrae is formed from a finely tooled galvanite alloy, while that of Clan Company Raukaan is black sigilanium veined with Theldrite circuitry. It is said that the Forgechain serves to remind its owner of the bonds that bind the Chapter together and the unbreakable strength they gain through unity. Yet there are those who believe its true purpose is to echo the chains that Ferrus Manus first bound around the fiery hearts of the Iron Hands, and that it serves as a reminder to all that true strength lies in restraint.*

# The Hall of Conquest

### c.M31 The Forging
In the wake of the Horus Heresy, the Legions of the First Founding are divided into smaller Chapters in accordance with the Codex Astartes. The surviving clan companies of the old Legion are divided amongst the Iron Hands and their successor Chapters, with the Iron Hands retaining the ten great clans of Medusa for their own. Company Raukaan are named for an especially warlike great clan who earned notoriety in the days before Ferrus Manus with their widespread, violent raiding.

### 807.M31 The Ulmetrican Reach Campaign

### 216.M34 The Beta Blockade
While tasked with enforcing the quarantine zone against the horrifying phenomenon known as the Pale Wasting, Clan Company Raukaan ruthlessly exterminate numerous fleeing bands of xenos, as well as the entirety of the Yormethi 26th Imperial Guard regiment.

### c.M35 Raukaan Undivided
During the shadowy events of the Moirae Schism, Clan Raukaan remain staunch and lose not a single battle-brother to the heretical doctrine.

### 550.M37 Logic Occluded
The heretic forces of the Occlusiad, servants of the deranged Archmagos who calls himself the Blind King, plunge a whole segmentum into war. Despite doctrinal wranglings within the Iron Council, Clan Company Raukaan are led into battle against the Blind King's forces time and again. Fighting under the leadership of Iron Father Daarmos, the warriors of Clan Company Raukaan win several notable victories including the Conflagration of Gold and the Bonehouse Massacre.

### 921.M40 A Disastrous Choice
Clan Raukaan are defending the Myrmidia System from Waaagh! Skullsmasha when they receive a distress call from the freighter *Endymion*, which reveals the Emperor's Children's presence. In response, Iron Father Daarmos leads Clan Raukaan in pursuit, but the distress call is a trap, and the Sapphire King's worshippers decimate Daarmos' force amid the bone jungles of Skarvus.

### 929.M40 Old Values
The staunchly conservative Iron Father Kristos is assigned to Clan Company Raukaan in the wake of the battle on Skarvus. Kristos and his old comrade, Iron Captain Graevaar, begin a regime of retraining and re-indoctrination to do away with the last traces of loyalty to Daarmos' demonstrably faulty leadership.

### 050.M41 Death on Dawnbreak
The restored Clan Company Raukaan leads a hammerblow Imperial offensive against Eldar forces on the planet of Dawnbreak. The Iron Hands show no interest in aiding other Imperial forces on the planet, instead securing their own, far more mysterious objectives before departing once more and leaving their 'allies' to their fate.

### 123.M41 The Cost of Victory
Several squads from Clan Company Raukaan, fighting under the leadership of Iron Captain Graevaar, crush a band of Dark Eldar slavers who have been striking at the vital agri worlds of the Hundhar Cluster. Several hundred agri-labourers are killed during the fighting; the Iron Hands, accused of using the civilians to bait an ambush, explaining afterwards that this was simply the most expedient course of action.

### 187.M41 A Reasonable Massacre
On the planet Dyronos, an armoured spearhead from Clan Raukaan are the first to break through the battle-lines of the Iron Warriors Warsmith, Lhon'Shul. Confronted with a sprawling prison facility, the Iron Hands find that the Warsmith's warriors have been mentally reconditioning captured Imperial Guard forces, turning the broken soldiers into fanatical Chaos Cultists. Rather than countenance any risk of taint, the Iron Hands systematically exterminate every living thing in the facility, traitors and captive loyalists alike. Despite the towering cost in potentially innocent lives, Clan Raukaan's actions are lauded by Inquisitors of the Ordo Malleus assigned to the war zone.

### 249.M41 The Weirdwaaagh!
A massive Ork Waaagh! descends upon the forge world Columnus. The Iron Hands assist the planet's defenders, Clan Company Raukaan eventually proving instrumental in the defeat of the Weirdwaagh! However, in the war's aftermath questions arise in the Iron Council regarding Iron Father Kristos' questionable conduct.

### 260.M41 The Calling of the Kristosian Conclave

### 272.M41 The Godsforge
Battling a Thousand Sons traitor warband amidst the ornately embellished caverns of the relic world of Dorloth II, a strikeforce of warriors from Clan Companies Raukaan, Garrsak and Dorrvok stumble across a mighty secret.

In a series of cavernous underground chambers they find a long lost forge complex, a relic of the earliest days of the Mechanicum. Though the Chapter turns their discovery over to the Martian Priesthood soon enough, they retain several artefacts for their own use, including the Mindforge Stave and the Gorgon's Chain.

### 364.M41 The War of Cogs

Clan Raukaan face a massive, boiler-driven horde of crude Ork war-constructs on the planet Faustin. Battles rage in the streets of Faustin's many cities, Raukaan Dreadnoughts and Centurions engaging in crushing, close-range brawls with the hordes of cog-driven and steam-belching greenskin machines.

### 460.M41 Obsession's Snare

A vast host of Iron Hands descends upon the Gaudinia System. Clan Company Raukaan once again takes the lead in a massive planetary assault upon Gaudania Prime and so is at the heart of the abominable trap that is there unleashed.

### 492.M41 A Sudden Reprieve

Clan Company Raukaan go into battle alongside the Cadian 832nd Infantry on the shadowed world of Cha'aun. After the Cadian advance becomes over-extended, it seems certain they will be overrun by the Ork forces. However, Iron Chaplain Shulgaar leads a counter-attack aboard the Land Raider *Iron Blade*, pushing the greenskins back long enough for the Imperial Guard to retreat with minimal casualties.

### 499.M41 The War on Balorian X

The planet of Balorian X is all but overrun by a Nurgle-worshipping Chaos cult. The ships of Clan Company Raukaan arrive at the vital moment, launching a series of punishing drop-assaults that scour the droning hordes from the face of the world and save the lives of many thousands of Imperial citizens.

### 587.M41 Of Angels and Iron

At the battle of Yawlen's Chasm, Master of the Forge Feirros leads warriors from Clan Raukaan into battle alongside a contingent of Blood Angels. The methodical, logically applied fire patterns of the Iron Hands combine with the noble heroics of the Blood Angels to crush a large force of Night Lords traitor Space Marines. In the battle's wake the two Chapters exchange solemn vows of support and allegiance.

### 751.M41 In the Shadows of Giants

Clan Raukaan are amongst the Iron Hands sent to the defence of Estaban II. There they fight once again alongside the mighty engines of Legio Tempestor, whose respect the clan company earned during the grim days of the Occlusiad. Between them, the Iron Hands and Titans win a mighty victory over a hellforged horde of Daemon Engines.

### 765.M41 Bromoch's Fate

Under the leadership of Iron Father Kardan Stronos, Clan Company Raukaan lend their strength to the war on the planet of Bromoch.

### 900.M41 Steel and Flame

Led by Kardan Stronos, a mighty force of Iron Hands and Brazen Claws attacks a Necron dynasty on the planet Shemnoch. While Stronos leads clan Garrsak in a headlong assault against the Necrons' leader, Clan Company Raukaan face the wrath of a Transcendent C'tan. Set loose by the Necrons in an act of desperation, this burning star-god scythes through the Iron Hands' ranks, hurling tanks through the air like toys and blasting battle-brothers to ash. It is finally brought low when Venerable Furnous coordinates the clan company's Dreadnoughts into a single unstoppable wave and charges the raging god. Though several of the Chapter's most ancient and venerated heroes fall, in the end the C'tan's blazing form is torn apart in a blaze of cosmic energies, leaving the victorious warriors of Clan Raukaan bloodied but unbowed.

### 934.M41 The War for Sylphas IV

Deployed upon a world of shifting silver and crystalline isles, elements of clan Raukaan find themselves in the midst of a war between the Eldar of Craftworld Il-Kaithe and a seemingly endless tide of Tzeentchian Daemons. An uneasy alliance follows, as the Iron Hands join forces with the craftworlders to drive the tide of gibbering Warpspawn back into the empyrean.

### 945.M41 A Rising Threat

The Iron Council note an alarming increase in Ork attacks throughout the galaxy. Each Calculum Rationale performed in response to these Ork attacks cogitates the need for an increasingly heavy-handed response. There are mutters among the Iron Fathers that – should this pattern continue – the Orks may soon become a logically untenable foe for the Iron Hands to face.

### 963.M41 A Stolen Tithe

Several of the Iron Hands' most commonly tithed recruiting worlds descend into anarchy and uproar. Their governors claim that the Iron Hands have been taking vast, unsustainable tithes of their populace, stealing them away in the dead of night. Efforts are made by the people of these worlds to resist recruitment, drawing the Iron Hands' wrath and leading to several brief and brutally one-sided wars.

Only after the smoke clears does the truth emerge. Bands of grotesquely warped Eldar pirates have in fact been responsible for the mass abductions, stealing the planets' peoples away into yawning portals. Chaplain Shulgaar assembles a strikeforce from Raukaan's ranks and successfully intercepts the next raid, punishing the xenos for their brazen temerity. The damage has already been done, however, and the Iron Hands' recruitment rate drops by almost a quarter over the next decade.

### 982.M41 Might of Medusa

A splinter of Hive Fleet Leviathan is detected making for the forge world of Grammachus Beta. Echoing their picket duties of so many millennia before, Clan Raukaan heads up a sizeable force of Iron Hands who race to the planet's defence. Though the fighting is fierce, the forge world is once again saved by the efforts of the Iron Hands, this time without undue loss of innocent lives.

### 999.M41 The Grand Calculation Begins

# COLOURS OF CONQUEST

Grim-faced Iron Captain armed with power sword and combi-grav

Clan Raukaan Master of the Forge

Details of iconography and servo-harness

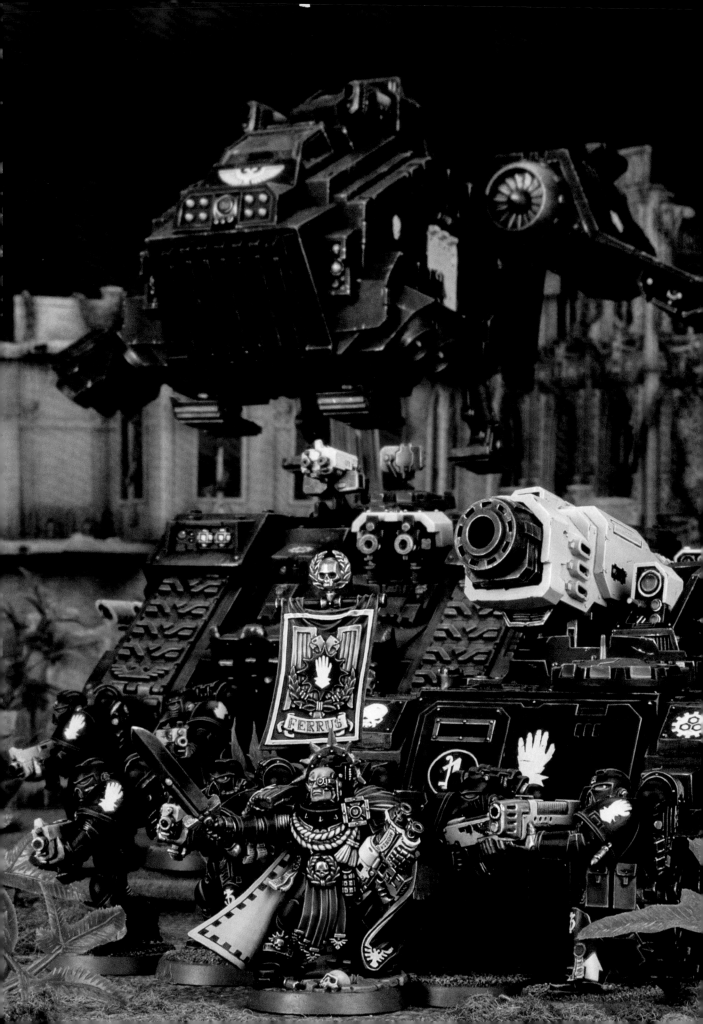

*Iron Hands Sternguard*

*Sternguard of Clan Company Avernii*

This Hunter bears the iconography of Clan Raukaan.

*Hunter of Clan Company Raukaan*

*A Tactical Squad of Clan Company Raukaan advance, with a Hunter guarding against aerial attack.*

*Clan Raukaan Sergeant with power sword*

*Tactical Marine with plasma gun*

*Battle-brother in Mk VI power armour*

*Battle-brothers of Clan Company Raukaan*

*Clan Raukaan Tactical Marines deploy from a Land Raider.*

*Clan Company Raukaan boasts the might of many ancient and deadly Dreadnoughts.*

# FORGING THE CLAN COMPANY

On the preceding pages you've read about the mighty battles of Clan Company Raukaan – now it's your turn to unleash their mechanical fury upon the field of war. When used alongside *Codex: Space Marines*, this section of the book contains everything you need to transform your collection of Space Marines into Librarian Lydriik and Iron Chaplain Shulgaar's cold, deadly warriors.

## HOW THIS SECTION WORKS

Within these pages, you will find:

### CLAN RAUKAAN

These pages present all of the alterations and additions to the rules given in *Codex: Space Marines* that you will need to transform your collection of Citadel miniatures into an army based on Clan Company Raukaan at any point during its long, bloody history.

- Crush your foes with the armoured might of Clan Raukaan's Dreadnoughts.

- Bolster your forces with cadres of Techmarines, enabling your engines of war to roll inexorably over the foe in the face of the heaviest fire.

- Equip your characters with the relics wielded by Epistolary Lydriik, Iron Chaplain Shulgaar and other heroes of Clan Company Raukaan.

- Use the Clan Company Raukaan Apocalypse datasheet to replicate the 3rd Company in all its relentless might.

### THE GORGON'S FORGE

*Even after the arrival of the Iron Hands, their home world remained sparsely developed, with much of the Medusan populace continuing their nomadic existence aboard vast, armoured crawlers. However, the Chapter does maintain a number of fortified facilities across the planet's surface, each serving purposes both practical and symbolic. One such location is the Gorgon's Forge, a vast factory complex located near Medusa's southern pole. Playing host to a contingent of Adeptus Mechanicus Tech-priests and rumoured to house a handful of STC fragments, the Gorgon's Forge rings day and night with the clamour of heavy industry. It is here that Iron Hands vehicles damaged during battle are brought to undergo repairs, and that the majority of the Chapter's Dreadnought sarcophagi lay at rest between battles. Here also are wrought the finest weapons of the Chapter, masterwork examples of the armourer's art constructed specifically for use by the Iron Hands' mightiest heroes.*

### CITIES OF DEATH & PLANETSTRIKE STRATAGEMS

Here you'll find additional stratagems for your Clan Raukaan army to use in games of Cities of Death. Wield weapons and tactics honed across ten thousand years of crushing armoured offensives and high-impact warfare. Claim buildings to house vehicle repair stations, direct your forces with mechanical precision or crush your foes with heavy armoured drop assaults.

### ALTAR OF WAR MISSIONS

Hone your battle-skills as you lead Clan Raukaan in a series of engagements crafted to match their fighting style. Do you have what it takes to master the Iron Hands' way of war?

- **Calculated Victory:** Smash the enemy within optimal parameters, not merely defeating them but ensuring their utter, efficient destruction.

- **Crush the Weak:** Prove the might of your warriors by exterminating the contemptible weaklings fielded by the foe. Let only the strong survive!

- **Logic Abandoned:** Once unfettered, the fury of Clan Company Raukaan is terrible to behold. Can you master this doubly-dangerous weapon of war?

### ECHOES OF WAR MISSIONS

Recreate pivotal battles from the history of Clan Raukaan. Lead the clan company from the defiant massacre on Skarvus, through the fires of a hard won redemption and into a new, more hopeful age.

- **Ambush on Skarvus:** Amid the bone jungles of the death world Skarvus, Clan Raukaan find themselves trapped in a deadly ambush by the Emperor's Children. Will the warriors of Clan Raukaan fight their way free, or will they perish and be forgotten?

- **The Hammer Falls:** Descend from the skies to purge the perfidious Eldar from the dig site on Dawnbreak, and claim the riches that lie below.

- **Ruthless Logic:** As the battle for the forge world of Columnus comes to a head, will you have the cold determination to win victory at any cost?

- **An Ancient Evil Revealed:** A trap many millennia in the making is finally sprung on the world of Gaudinia Prime. Yet Clan Company Raukaan stand unbowed.

- **Iron and Steel:** Something terrible has risen to reclaim the world of Bromoch. The resurgent warriors of Clan Raukaan must lead the battle to annihilate this ancient foe, or die in the attempt.

# CLAN RAUKAAN AT WAR

A Clan Raukaan detachment is chosen using the army list presented in *Codex: Space Marines*. It also has a series of supplemental rules (presented below) that must be used in addition to the material found in *Codex: Space Marines*. When choosing a Clan Raukaan detachment, you may only use the Iron Hands Chapter Tactics.

## MARCH OF THE ANCIENTS

In a Clan Raukaan detachment, Dreadnoughts, Venerable Dreadnoughts and Ironclad Dreadnoughts may be taken as Heavy Support choices as well as Elites choices. Declare what type of choice each model is when it is deployed.

## SCIONS OF THE FORGE

For each HQ choice in a Clan Raukaan detachment (not including other Techmarines, Servitors, Command Squads or Honour Guard) you may include up to two Techmarines. For each Master of the Forge in your army, you may include up to three Techmarines. These selections do not use up a Force Organisation slot.

## GIFTS OF THE GORGON

Any character in your Clan Raukaan detachment that can select Chapter Relics cannot select from those listed in *Codex: Space Marines*, but can instead select from the Gifts of the Gorgon on page 50, at the points cost shown.

## WARLORD TRAITS

When generating his Warlord Traits, a Clan Raukaan Warlord can either roll on one of the Warlord Traits tables in the *Warhammer 40,000* rulebook, or roll on the table on the right.

## WARLORD TRAITS

| D6 | RESULT |
|---|---|
| 1 | **Adept of the Omnissiah:** *There are few, even amongst the Iron Hands, that can commune with machine spirits with greater skill than this Warlord.* Your Warlord has the Blessing of the Omnissiah special rule (see *Codex: Space Marines*) If the Warlord already has this special rule, he may re-roll any failed attempts to repair a vehicle. |
| 2 | **Will of Iron:** *Even under the most desperate circumstances, this Warlord's courage remains as unyielding as adamantium.* Your Warlord has the Fearless special rule. |
| 3 | **Flesh is Weak:** *This Warlord bears such an extraordinary amount of cybernetic enhancements that he is more machine than man.* Your Warlord adds +1 to any Feel No Pain rolls he makes. |
| 4 | **Student of History:** *Well aware of his Primarch's failure on Isstvan V, this Warlord's cold logic is such that he knows only too well when to fight on and when it is best to withdraw.* Your Warlord, and any Clan Raukaan unit he joins, can choose to automatically fail any Morale check it is required to make |
| 5 | **Merciless Resolve:** *To the Iron Hands, mercy is for the weak, and there are few finer proponents of this adage than this pitiless Warlord.* Your Warlord, and all friendly Clan Raukaan units within 12", have the Crusader special rule |
| 6 | **Target Protocols:** *This Warlord uses his advanced augmetics to direct the fire of his battle-brothers and efficiently distribute targeting data to those about him.* Your Warlord, and any Clan Raukaan unit he joins, re-roll To Hit rolls of a 1 in the Shooting phase. |

# GIFTS OF THE GORGON

The Gifts of the Gorgon are revered artefacts and trophies of war borne into battle by Clan Company Raukaan. Only one of each of the following relics can be chosen per army – there is only one of each of these items in the entire galaxy!

## THE MINDFORGE STAVE .................................. 15 POINTS

*Crafted with gene-keyed psychocircuitry, the Mindforge Stave possesses a rudimentary machine-spirit sentience. Through ancient techno-sorcery now long lost, the stave imprints with an individual suitably endowed with both psychic mastery and cybernetic augmentation. Epistolary Lydriis was the first to take up the stave upon its discovery, and the weapon has bound itself irrevocably to him. He has wielded it ever since. In battle, the Mindforge Stave allows the wielder to channel the might of his mind into white-hot sledgehammer blows that smash foes from their feet or crush them to pulp with a single swing.*

The Mindforge Stave can only be carried by a Librarian, and replaces his force weapon.

| Range | S | AP | Type |
|---|---|---|---|
| - | x2 | 2 | Melee, Concussive, Force, Unwieldy |

## THE AXE OF MEDUSA ......................................... 25 POINTS

*Traditionally the Axe of Medusa has been held by the Iron Council and given to the Chapter's chosen war leader as a badge of office. For over three centuries now this weapon has been wielded by Kardan Stronos, and used to great effect in battle. However, when dispatching another hero of the Iron Hands on some particularly important mission, Stronos has been known to bestow the Axe of Medusa as a mark of favour and faith.*

| Range | S | AP | Type |
|---|---|---|---|
| - | +2 | 2 | Melee, Master-crafted, Severing Strike, Unwieldy. |

**Severing Strike:** Each time the bearer of the Axe of Medusa rolls a 6 To Hit, resolve that attack at +4 Strength instead. Any other hits are resolved at +2 Strength as normal.

## THE IRONSTONE ................................................. 30 POINTS

*The device must be mag-clamped to the gorget of the bearer, where it gathers power from his armour, gradually awakening the cluster of potent machine spirits that lurk within its coldly glowing shell. When a vehicle nearby suffers battle-damage, the Magos-class machine spirits within the Ironstone will surge out, possessing the wounded machine and swiftly repairing the damage.*

Friendly Clan Raukaan Tanks and Walkers within 6" of the bearer pass their It Will Not Die rolls on a 4+. If this roll is a 6, the Ironstone also repairs a Weapon Destroyed or Immobilised result that the vehicle suffered earlier in the battle (controlling player's choice).

## BETRAYER'S BANE ............................................. 25 POINTS

*This combi-weapon contains an auto-sanctified thermal generator that replenishes its fuel reserves as the battle goes on. Its case is inscribed with the name of every battlefield upon which it has slain warriors of the Emperor's Children, and serves as a potent symbol of vengeance.*

| | Range | S | AP | Type |
|---|---|---|---|---|
| Boltgun barrel | 24" | 4 | 5 | Rapid Fire, Master-crafted |
| Melta barrel | 12" | 8 | 1 | Assault 1, Master-crafted, Melta |

## THE GORGON'S CHAIN ...................................... 45 POINTS

*Far from being an actual, physical chain, this small augmetic module is fitted within its owner's armour, linking through his black carapace and extending monomolecular mechadendrites into his twin hearts. Thus connected, it draws power from its owner to generate a potent protective field. Only as the bearer's wounds become too great to sustain will the Gorgon's Chain unravel.*

The bearer of the Gorgon's Chain has the following special rules, depending on how many unsaved Wounds he has suffered during the battle:

| Wounds Suffered | Special Rules |
|---|---|
| 0 | The bearer has a 3+ invulnerable save, +1 to his Feel No Pain rolls and the Eternal Warrior special rule. |
| 1 | The bearer has a 3+ invulnerable save and the Eternal Warrior special rule. |
| 2 | The bearer has a 3+ invulnerable save. |
| 3 | The bearer has a 4+ invulnerable save. |

Each time the bearer suffers an unsaved Wound or recovers a Wound as a result of the It Will Not Die special rule, the effects of the Gorgon's Chain change immediately; you should roll the bearer's saves individually.

## THE TEMPERED HELM ....................................... 35 POINTS

*The savant-possessor within this helmet filters incoming information and presents it in compartmentalised strategic sermons to its wearer, granting a near-omnipotent level of instant battlefield cognition. The helm also permits its wearer to override vox signals and targeting augurs with their own commands, so the wearer enjoys unparalleled control over his forces.*

When taking Morale tests, all friendly units within 24" of the bearer can use his Leadership characteristic instead of their own. Furthermore, nominate a single friendly unit within 12" of the bearer at the start of each of his Shooting phases. That unit can re-roll all To Hit rolls of a 1 in that Shooting phase. Both of these rules can be used even if the bearer is embarked in a vehicle or building.

# APOCALYPSE
# CLAN COMPANY RAUKAAN

*When Clan Company Raukaan deploy as a single force there are few foes in the galaxy that can stay their wrath. Fully embracing the teachings of Kardan Stronos, the battle-brothers of Clan Raukaan fight with a tempered balance of cold logic and restrained wrath that makes them truly deadly foes. Furthermore, the masters of Clan Company Raukaan can call upon the might of their personal armoury, reinforcing their forces with Dreadnoughts, Centurions, and battle tanks. So augmented, Clan Raukaan tends naturally towards sledgehammer armoured offensives, grinding the foe beneath the tracks of their many tanks before deploying their infantry assets to crush whatever remains. Once an attack of this sort has gathered momentum it is almost unstoppable, punching through defence lines to annihilate command assets or seize crucial objectives that the enemy believed well behind the lines of battle.*

1 Captain

1 Chaplain

3 Techmarines

1 Command Squad

6 Tactical Squads

2 Devastator Squads

1 Assault Squad

1 Centurion Assault Squad

3 Dreadnoughts (of any type)

1 Predator

1 Vindicator

1 Hunter

### FORMATION RESTRICTIONS
All Tactical, Devastator and Assault Squads must include the maximum number of models possible.

**SPECIAL RULES:**

**Comrades-in-Arms:** If an enemy unit declares a charge against a unit in this formation, then any unengaged non-vehicle units from this formation within 12" of the charging unit's target can choose to fire Overwatch as if they were also targets of the charge (though they can still only fire Overwatch once per phase).

**No Weakness, No Mercy:** All models in this formation re-roll To Wound and Armour Penetration rolls of 1. This applies to both shooting and close combat attacks.

**Seize and Control:** All units in the formation within 12" of a Strategic Objective have the **Stubborn** special rule.

**Strike Cruiser:** The player with this formation has an additional Orbital Strike Strategic Asset.

# CITIES OF DEATH STRATAGEMS

These are additional stratagems for Cities of Death games. They can be used if you are using the supplemental rules given in the Clan Raukaan at War section (pg 49). To do so, simply add them to the list of available stratagems.

## KEY BUILDINGS STRATAGEMS

### Vehicle Repair Hub

*In order to support their frequent use of Dreadnoughts and tanks in urban combat, Clan Raukaan often commandeers suitable buildings to act as temporary repair stations. These hubs are manned by a handful of tech-servitors, enslaved to the will of a Techmarine who remotely controls their actions from his location by means of a highly advanced neural impulse cogitator. As nearby vehicles suffer battle damage, these tech-servitors mindlessly plod into the fray to effect battlefield repairs, oblivious to any danger to themselves.*

Friendly Clan Raukaan vehicles within 6" of the Vehicle Repair Hub pass their It Will Not Die rolls on a 4+.

## DIRTY TRICKS STRATAGEMS

### Mechanical Precision

*Even amongst the Adeptus Astartes, whose military organisation is legend across the universe, the Iron Hands are renowned for the impeccable timing of the arrival of their reserve assets. The Iron Hands do not engage the foe without meticulous research and preparation beforehand, the fruits of such labour distributed to every battle-brother via simulus chamber inloads. As a result, there are few eventualities in battle that Clan Raukaan has not already predicted and taken steps to counter in turn.*

The Clan Raukaan player can re-roll Reserve rolls.

### Rapid Advance

*Despite their unique heritage, Clan Raukaan are Space Marines first and foremost. The Adeptus Astartes are rightly feared for their ability to switch seamlessly from defence to attack in the midst of a battle, often wrong-footing the enemy and exploiting that advantage to inflict heavy casualties.*

One use only. At the start of his turn, the Clan Raukaan player selects one special rule from the following list: Crusader, Move Through Cover or Relentless. The nominated special rule applies to all friendly, non-vehicle Clan Raukaan units for the duration of that turn.

### Orbital Strike

*Space Marines are masters of planetary assaults. Long after establishing a beachhead on the planet's surface, they maintain constant lines of communication to their Strike Cruisers and Battle Barges in orbit. Should they find the enemy entrenched, a Clan Raukaan commander will call upon one of his clan's ships to unleash deadly bombardments from low orbit, obliterating the Emperor's foes with overwhelming force.*

One use only. Your Warlord can call down an Orbital Bombardment as if he was a Chapter Master (see *Codex: Space Marines*). If your Warlord is also a Chapter Master, this stratagem allows you to fire one additional Orbital Bombardment during the course of the game, though they cannot be fired on the same turn.

## ARMOURY STRATAGEMS

### Special Issue Ammunition

*Each and every squad of Space Marines is an elite fighting unit. As such, any squad can be assigned a dangerous battlefield role and be expected to carry it out without question or complaint. However, some of these missions may require the use of specialist wargear or equipment. Masters of preparation and planning, the warriors of Clan Company Raukaan have vast reserves of munitions to match the weaknesses of every foe, even beyond the fearsome array of weaponry normally utilised by the Space Marines.*

Nominate one friendly, non-vehicle Clan Raukaan unit and select one type of special issue ammunition from the following list: dragonfire bolts, hellfire rounds, kraken bolts or vengeance rounds. The nominated unit replaces their boltgun weapon profile (including boltguns that are part of a combi-weapon or mounted on a Space Marine bike) with the appropriate special issue ammunition profile described in *Codex: Space Marines*.

## OBSTACLES STRATAGEMS

### Ammunition Caches

*When Space Marines wage war, they do so equipped with enough stores of ammunition to fight for many months without resupply. If forced to engage the foe in a static combat theatre, a Space Marine commander will often order caches of ammunition to be placed in strategic locations, providing a surplus of munitions to supply any squads tasked with defending those areas, allowing them to maintain a punishing rate of fire almost without end.*

The Clan Raukaan player can deploy D3 ammunition caches anywhere on the table. Each ammunition cache follows all of the rules for an Ammunition Dump (see the *Warhammer 40,000* rulebook).

## DEPLOYMENT STRATAGEMS

### Heavy Armour Drop

*The Iron Hands have developed a number of ways to drop armoured vehicles and Dreadnoughts behind enemy lines, where they can engage the enemy from an unexpected quarter. Most commonly, they will utilise Thunderhawk Transporters or Drop Pods to deploy their revered ancients. However, inventive Clan Raukaan Techmarines have trialed other, more esoteric means of deploying armour, such as high-altitude vehicle drops using powerful anti-grav thrusters that detach upon landing, or even large scale teleportation hangars that can transfer an entire tank squadron to the planet's surface within the space of a few heartbeats. These more outlandish methods have yet to be perfected, forcing the Iron Hands to deploy their precious cargo outside of the immediate combat theatre lest they prove unacceptably vulnerable upon arrival.*

The Clan Raukaan player can nominate up to D3 Tanks (other than Transports or Dedicated Transports) or Dreadnoughts to have the Outflank special rule.

# PLANETSTRIKE STRATAGEMS

These are additional stratagems for Planetstrike games. They can be used if you are using the supplemental rules given in the Clan Raukaan at War section (pg 49). To do so, simply add them to the list of available stratagems.

## ATTACK STRATAGEMS

### Relentless Bombardment      Stratagem Points: 1
**When declared: Immediately before the firestorm**

*Clan Company Raukaan never hold back when they fight a war. Many of their warships also sport an even more ferocious arsenal of bombardment weaponry than those utilised by most Adeptus Astartes ships, shattering their foes before the true storm of death begins.*

The Clan Raukaan player adds an additional D3+1 to the number of Firestorm attacks he makes.

### Overwhelming Firepower      Stratagem Points: 2
**When declared: Immediately after the firestorm**

*When the warriors of Clan Raukaan deploy into a combat theatre, they do so in great force. To reinforce the brutality of their assault, each squad is equipped with extra boltgun ammunition to expend during their deployment. This enables the Iron Hands to maintain a terrifying rate of fire in the first few moments of their assault, blasting apart countless enemies with their punishing bolter storm.*

All friendly Clan Raukaan non-vehicle units that deploy via Deep Strike (or disembark from a Deep-striking vehicle) can fire an additional shot on the turn they arrive with any bolt pistol, boltgun, storm bolter or heavy bolter. This bonus shot also applies to boltguns that are part of a combi-weapon as well as boltguns that are within rapid fire range of their targets (for a total of 3 shots).

### Clockwork Precision      Stratagem Points: 1
**When declared: At the beginning of any of your turns.**

*Space Marines overwhelm their foe with the precise application of overwhelming force. So effective is the military organisation laid out in the Codex Astartes that all Chapters are capable of launching combined arms assaults with astonishing precision. Clan Raukaan's mastery of this doctrine is undisputed, making a mockery of the notion that plans rarely survive contact with the enemy.*

For the duration of the turn in which this stratagem is used, you may re-roll each of your unsuccessful Reserve Rolls. Furthermore, you may re-roll the scatter dice for each unit that Deep Strikes into play this turn.

### Destruction Protocols      Stratagem Points: 2
**When declared: At the beginning of any of your turns.**

*During their years of training, Space Marines learn to determine the weak spots of a building with but a glance. Should the situation call for the destruction of an enemy structure above all else, this training will rise to the fore, and the enemy will soon learn how foolish they were to believe themselves safe behind their armoured walls.*

Nominate a single building. For the duration of the turn in which this stratagem is used, all friendly Clan Raukaan units re-roll failed armour penetration rolls against the nominated building. Affected units may also re-roll glancing hits in an attempt to get a penetrating hit, though you must accept the result of the second roll, even if it is worse than the first.

## DEFENCE STRATAGEMS

### Skyfire Targeting Cogitator      Stratagem Points: 1
**When declared: After you have deployed your units.**

*Mastery of advanced technology is second nature to the Techmarines of the Iron Hands. Such is their innate skill that they can retrofit battlefield archeotech to serve their Chapter's purpose should the calculated predictions of the Iron Fathers deem such actions to be advantageous. If Clan Raukaan expects an aerial or orbital threat, a common example of this modification will be a rudimentary targeting cogitator hub which enables the warriors nearby to coordinate effective anti-aircraft fire.*

Nominate one Planetstrike Objective. Do not roll on the Mysterious Objective table for this Planetstrike Objective – instead it is automatically a Skyfire Nexus (see the *Warhammer 40,000* rulebook).

### Ironclad      Stratagem Points: 1
**When declared: After you have deployed your units.**

*The Iron Hands are amongst the most stoic of Space Marine Chapters, their cold, calculated determination all but impossible to overcome. Should they be forced to dig in and repel an enemy assault, the Iron Hands will look to their highly skilled Masters of the Forge and Techmarines to fortify their defences. If logic dictates that a specific building will form the key component of their defensive strategy, these ingenious engineers will clad its flanks in specially-crafted layers of obstinite, reinforcing its structure to resist all but the heaviest damage.*

Nominate one building. That building's Armour Value is increased by 1 point on all facings, to a maximum Armour Value of 15.

### Valiant Stand      Stratagem Points: 2
**When declared: After you have deployed your units.**

*The Space Marines are one of the most determined fighting forces in the galaxy. Though the Emperor's Angels of Death are famed for launching precision strikes and rapid orbital assaults, when circumstances force them to plant their feet and hold position against an overwhelming foe, there are few more daunting enemies to face in battle. The warriors of Clan Company Raukaan exemplify this trait, forming an impenetrable wall of steel against which almost any foe will break.*

All friendly Clan Raukaan units within 6" of a Planetstrike Objective have the Stubborn special rule.

# CLAN RAUKAAN

## INTRODUCTION

The *Warhammer 40,000* rulebook already includes a set of Eternal War missions; when you multiply that by the different armies you might face, and the myriad different ways you can set up the terrain for your battle, there are hundreds, probably thousands of different ways to play. However, we feel that you can never have too much variety, so this book has three new missions you can use if you or an opponent has a Clan Raukaan army.

The new missions illustrate the different sorts of strategies used by Clan Raukaan, and they will provide new tests of your tactical ability as a commander. Additional Altar of War mission books have scenarios for use by other armies from the Warhammer 40,000 galaxy.

## STRATEGY

Different armies use different strategies when they go to war, which affects the types of battle that they fight. The Black Templars, for example, hurl themselves at their foes to engage them in savage melees where their ferocity and zealous determination often earns them a swift and bloody victory. Meanwhile, the disciplined warriors of the Tau Empire utilise their highly advanced technology and tactical flexibility to cut their enemies down at a distance, believing close combat to be crude and uncivilised. It takes a skilled general to learn the strengths and weaknesses of their forces, and to employ them effectively whatever the scenario.

The missions found here are themed around the stoic Clan Company Raukaan and the way they fight. This gives you a chance to discover more about the strategies used by the Iron Hands 3rd Company, and then to try these strategies out on the tabletop. It also means that the army you command can affect the types of battle you are likely to fight. This is highly appropriate – after all, you would expect to fight a very different sort of battle as an Iron Father than you would as an Ork Warlord.

## TACTICS

The three Altar of War missions included in this book are designed to provide players with games that will really challenge their tactical ability. We've gone to some pains to make sure that each mission is as balanced as possible, and that they provide both sides with a new set of tactical challenges to overcome.

This means that, in order to win, you will need to be prepared to think on your feet and quickly adapt to the new circumstances the missions will throw at you.

You may be called upon to spearhead an attack or fight to hold a defensive position deep behind enemy lines. Tried and trusted tactics will need to be re-thought in the face of these new challenges, and you will need to be ready to think outside the box in order to win.

## A GALAXY OF WEAKNESS TO PURGE

That, then, is what this section is all about, and on the following pages you will find out how to put these ideas into practice on your gaming table. We'll start off with an overview of how to incorporate the new missions into the games you play, and then we'll provide the missions themselves. You'll also find plenty of background information about of how the armies fight and how the missions we've provided fit into their strategic battle plans.

## HOW TO USE ALTAR OF WAR MISSIONS

The Altar of War Missions part of this book is split into two sections: the section that you are reading now, which explains how to incorporate the Altar of War: Clan Raukaan missions into your games of Warhammer 40,000, and the missions themselves.

It is very straightforward to use an Altar of War mission – it only requires a handful of minor modifications to the rules for fighting a battle in the *Warhammer 40,000* rulebook. These changes are explained in detail on the following page, but they boil down to: roll-off if you want to use an Altar of War mission; if you win, you can roll on an Altar of War mission table instead of the Eternal War mission table. And that's it!

## THE MISSION

If either you or your opponent wish to use an Altar of War mission, then you must make a roll-off at the start of The Mission step of Fighting A Battle (as described in the *Warhammer 40,000* rulebook).

The winner of the roll-off can choose either to roll on the Eternal War mission table, or instead roll on the Altar of War mission table for their army. Other supplements also have new types of mission tables, and the winner of the dice roll-off could choose to roll on one of those, if they prefer and are allowed to do so. These rolls will determine which mission is used for the battle. Note that each set of Altar of War missions is linked to an army chosen from a specific codex; in order to use Altar of War missions, an army chosen from the appropriate codex must be the primary detachment. In the case of Altar of War: Clan Raukaan, the missions are linked to armies chosen from *Codex: Space Marines* using the additional rules found in the Clan Raukaan at War section (pg 49)

For example, Andy and Simon have arranged to play a game of Warhammer 40,000. Andy has brought along his Clan Raukaan army and this book, while Simon is using his World Eaters Chaos Space Marines and has the Eternal War missions from the *Warhammer 40,000* rulebook. They roll-off and Andy wins. He decides to roll on the Clan Raukaan Mission table in this book. If Simon had won, he would have rolled on the Eternal War Mission table.

### ALTAR OF WAR: CLAN RAUKAAN MISSION TABLE

| D6 | Mission |
| --- | --- |
| 1-2 | Calculated Victory |
| 3-4 | Crush the Weak |
| 5-6 | Logic Abandoned |

## THE BATTLEFIELD

The deployment map, deployment zones and deployment instructions for each Altar of War: Clan Raukaan mission are included in the missions themselves; unless otherwise stated, do not use the deployment maps found in the *Warhammer 40,000* rulebook.

## THE ENEMY

The player that won the roll-off and rolled on the Altar of War Mission table is known as 'the Clan Raukaan player' in the rules and missions that follow, and their opponent is known as 'the enemy player'. Note that the player that loses the roll-off counts as 'the enemy' for the purposes of an Altar of War mission, even if they have a Clan Raukaan army too.

## RESERVES

Altar of War missions follow all of the rules for Reserves in the *Warhammer 40,000* rulebook; however, some specify different limits on how many units may (or must) be placed in Reserve rather than deployed at the start of the game.

## TO WAR!

These three changes aside, all of the rules for Fighting a Battle in the *Warhammer 40,000* rulebook are used as normal for the Altar of War missions.

## SELECTED BATTLE MISSIONS

*As an alternative to rolling on a mission table, you and your opponent can agree to choose the mission you wish to fight. Picking missions is a great way to try out a particular mission you haven't fought before or to hone your skills at missions you have previously fought.*

### ECHOES OF WAR

*After the Altar of War missions, you will find a selection of Echoes of War missions inspired by the battles fought by Clan Raukaan and related in this book. The Armies section of each of these missions provide guidance on the forces present so that you can replay the pivotal events using the armies, characters and war machines described in this book. Each Echoes of War mission includes a map that depicts the battlefield on which the conflicts were fought.*

*For those with a mind to historical accuracy, you'll notice certain restrictions and rules that we use to replicate the conditions of the battle in question. Whilst the Echoes of War missions have been inspired by specific events, with a little imagination they can easily be repurposed to recreate battles of your own invention. If you choose to go this route, you can modify these missions so that they can be fought using any combination of forces and terrain in your collection.*

# CALCULATED VICTORY

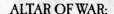

*'Victory is at its most efficient when it is absolute.'*

When the Iron Hands engage the enemy, it is ever with optimal efficiency in mind. This concept manifests itself in the statistical outcome of the victory: did the Iron Hands eliminate sufficient enemy targets whilst remaining within acceptable loss parameters? Was the enemy's leadership structure annihilated, or otherwise incapacitated enough to prevent organised reprisals within a specified time frame? Was the enemy force subjugated without the unnecessary deployment of high-level assets? All such data is examined and assessed by the Chapter's Iron Fathers to ensure that the Iron Hands fight at peak efficiency at all times.

Following these imperatives, the warriors of Clan Raukaan engage the enemy without hesitation or remorse, sure in their objectives and acutely aware of the manner in which their victory will be judged.

## THE ARMIES

Choose armies as described in the Fighting a Battle section of the *Warhammer 40,000* rulebook. The Clan Raukaan player must choose a primary detachment from *Codex: Space Marines* using the extra rules presented in this book.

## THE BATTLEFIELD

Use the deployment map included in this mission. Set up terrain as described in the Fighting a Battle section of the *Warhammer 40,000* rulebook.

## DEPLOYMENT

Players should first roll for Warlord Traits and then deploy as described in the Fighting a Battle section of the *Warhammer 40,000* rulebook.

## FIRST TURN

The player that deployed first has the first turn unless their opponent can Seize the Initiative as described in the *Warhammer 40,000* rulebook.

## GAME LENGTH

This scenario uses Variable Game Length as described in the *Warhammer 40,000* rulebook.

## VICTORY CONDITIONS

At the end of the game, the player who has scored the most Victory Points wins the game. If players have the same number of Victory Points, the game is a draw.

### PRIMARY OBJECTIVE

**At the end of the game, each player receives 1 Victory Point for each enemy unit that has been completely destroyed. However, players instead receive 2 Victory Points for each HQ or elites unit completely destroyed in this manner.** Units that are falling back at the end of the game, and units that are not on the board at the end of the game, count as destroyed for the purposes of this mission. Remember that Independent Characters and Dedicated Transports are individual units and award Victory Points if they are destroyed.

### SECONDARY OBJECTIVES

**Slay the Warlord\*, First Blood, Linebreaker.**

\* **In this mission, the Slay the Warlord Secondary Objective is worth 3 Victory Points.** Note that this includes the Victory Points earned as part of this mission's Primary Objective.

## MISSION SPECIAL RULES

**Night Fighting, Reserves.**

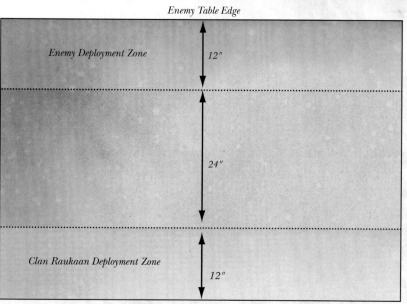

*Enemy Table Edge*

*Enemy Deployment Zone*

12"

24"

*Clan Raukaan Deployment Zone*

12"

*Clan Raukaan Table Edge*

# ALTAR OF WAR:
# CRUSH THE WEAK

*'These cowards have not the strength to live. We shall grant them freedom from this concern.'*

The Iron Hands are renowned – notorious even – for their unashamed contempt for those who cannot survive the many horrors of the universe by virtue of their own courage and strength. On many occasions, they have simply left their allies, or those that as Space Marines they are sworn to protect, to die if they cannot fend for themselves.

Yet the scorn that the Iron Hands hold for the weak is far from reserved for those they fight alongside – if anything, their disgust is magnified many times over when doing battle with their enemies. They advance in implacable ranks of black and iron into the meat grinder of war until only the strong are left alive. So does Clan Company Raukaan stand alone on yet another victorious battlefield.

## THE ARMIES
Choose armies as described in the Fighting a Battle section of the *Warhammer 40,000* rulebook. The Clan Raukaan player must choose a primary detachment from *Codex: Space Marines* using the extra rules presented in this book.

## THE BATTLEFIELD
Use the deployment map included in this mission. Set up terrain as described in the Fighting a Battle section of the *Warhammer 40,000* rulebook. This mission requires no objective markers.

## DEPLOYMENT
Players should first roll for Warlord Traits and then Deploy Forces as described in the Fighting a Battle section of the *Warhammer 40,000* rulebook.

## FIRST TURN
The player that deployed first has the first turn unless their opponent can Seize the Initiative as described in the *Warhammer 40,000* rulebook.

## GAME LENGTH
This scenario uses Variable Game Length as described in the Fighting a Battle section of the *Warhammer 40,000* rulebook.

## VICTORY CONDITIONS
If, at the end of any game turn, the enemy player has no models on the battlefield, the Clan Raukaan player wins. If the game ends before this condition has been met, the enemy player wins instead.

## MISSION SPECIAL RULES
**Night Fighting, Reserves.**

**Cometh the Executioners:** Every unit in the Clan Raukaan army has the Fear special rule.

**Press the Attack:** Each time a Clan Raukaan troops or Dreadnought unit (including Venerable and Ironclad Dreadnoughts) is completely destroyed, remove it from play and place it into Ongoing Reserves, where it will be available to return to the battle at the start of the Clan Raukaan player's next turn.

**Wild Despair:** Every unit in the enemy army has the Hatred special rule.

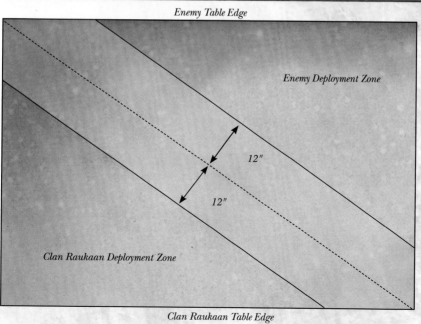

Enemy Table Edge

Enemy Deployment Zone

12"

12"

Clan Raukaan Deployment Zone

Clan Raukaan Table Edge

# ALTAR OF WAR:
# LOGIC ABANDONED

*'Let anger fuel your hearts, brothers. This is no time for cogitation. Attack!'*

Though they favour the use of reason and mechanical efficiency in all things to guide their actions, Clan Raukaan are no longer afraid of overriding their logic-based protocols if circumstances dictate the need for passion and fury. Many an enemy of the Chapter – including their daemonic anathema, the dreaded Sapphire King – has fallen foul of this uncharacteristic change in tack. Their sudden and unexpected emotional outburst grants the warriors of Clan Company Raukaan a spirited vitality as they pour forth their pent-up aggression and hatred into their blows, cutting down those that have angered them with terrible purpose until the source of their ire lies dead.

## THE ARMIES

Choose armies as described in the Fighting a Battle section of the *Warhammer 40,000* rulebook. The Clan Raukaan player must choose a primary detachment from *Codex: Space Marines* using the extra rules presented in this book.

## THE BATTLEFIELD

Use the deployment map included in this mission. Set up terrain as described in the Fighting a Battle section of the *Warhammer 40,000* rulebook. This mission requires no objective markers.

## DEPLOYMENT

Players should first roll for Warlord Traits and then Deploy Forces as described in the Fighting a Battle section of the *Warhammer 40,000* rulebook.

## FIRST TURN

The player that deployed first has the first turn unless their opponent can Seize the Initiative as described in the *Warhammer 40,000* rulebook.

## GAME LENGTH

This scenario uses Variable Game Length as described in the *Warhammer 40,000* rulebook.

## VICTORY CONDITIONS

At the end of the game, the player who has scored the most Victory Points wins the game. If players have the same number of Victory Points, the game is a draw.

## PRIMARY OBJECTIVE

**At the end of the game, each player receives 1 Victory Point for each enemy unit that has been completely destroyed.** Units that are falling back at the end of the game, and units that are not on the board at the end of the game count as destroyed for the purposes of this mission. Remember that Independent Characters and Dedicated Transports are individual units and award Victory Points if they are destroyed. Furthermore, the Clan Raukaan player can earn additional Victory Points as follows:

- If you slay the enemy Warlord, you score 1 Victory Point.
- If you slay the enemy Warlord in close combat, you instead score 2 Victory Points.
- If you slay the enemy Warlord in a challenge, you instead score 3 Victory Points.
- If your Warlord slays the enemy Warlord in close combat, you instead score 4 Victory Points.
- If your Warlord slays the enemy Warlord in a challenge, you instead score 5 Victory Points.
- If the enemy Warlord is alive at the end of the game (whether he is in Ongoing Reserves or not), you lose 3 Victory Points.

## SECONDARY OBJECTIVES
**Slay the Warlord\*, First Blood, Linebreaker.**

\* Only the enemy player can achieve this objective – the Clan Raukaan player earns Victory Points for slaying the enemy Warlord as described above.

## MISSION SPECIAL RULES
**Reserves, Night Fighting.**

**Fury of the Primarch:** All non-vehicle Clan Raukaan units have the Furious Charge and Hatred special rules, but cannot Go to Ground and cannot choose to fail a Morale check due to the Our Weapons Are Useless rule (see the *Warhammer 40,000* rulebook).

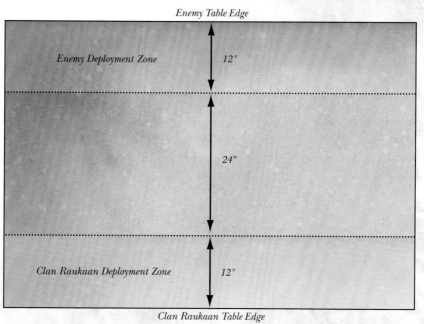

Enemy Table Edge

Enemy Deployment Zone 12"

24"

Clan Raukaan Deployment Zone 12"

Clan Raukaan Table Edge

# ECHOES OF WAR:
# AMBUSH ON SKARVUS

Lured away from their defence of the Myrmidia system by the promise of vengeance against a bitter foe, Clan Company Raukaan has made planetfall on the desiccated planet of Skarvus. Amid the bone-strewn death world, the Iron Hands track their quarry with uncharacteristically reckless hate and unwittingly fall into a trap that the Emperor's Children had carefully prepared for them.

Now surrounded on all sides, and against seemingly impossible odds, Clan Raukaan can do little but grit their teeth and vent their fury against their mortal enemies as their ambushers close in for the kill.

## THE ARMIES

Choose armies as described in the Fighting a Battle section of the *Warhammer 40,000* rulebook. The Clan Raukaan player must choose a primary detachment from *Codex: Space Marines* using the extra rules presented in this book. The enemy player must choose a primary detachment from *Codex: Chaos Space Marines*, and must include an HQ choice with the Mark of Slaanesh to be his Warlord, and at least two other units with the Mark of Slaanesh special rule.

## THE BATTLEFIELD

Use the deployment map included in this mission. Set up terrain as described in the Fighting a Battle section of the *Warhammer 40,000* rulebook. This mission requires no objective markers.

## DEPLOYMENT

Before any models are deployed, both players should roll to determine their Warlord Traits.

The Clan Raukaan player deploys first, placing all of his non-Flyer units in the deployment zone depicted on the map. The enemy player then deploys his units in either of the enemy deployment zones depicted on the map.

## FIRST TURN

The enemy player has the first turn.

## GAME LENGTH

This mission uses Variable Game Length as described in the *Warhammer 40,000* rulebook.

## VICTORY CONDITIONS

**At the end of the game, the Clan Raukaan player wins if he has any models remaining on the battlefield, including those in units that are falling back. If he has no models remaining, his opponent wins.** Units that are not on the board at the end of the game count as destroyed for the purposes of this mission.

## MISSION SPECIAL RULES

**Night Fighting, Reserves.**

**Emperor's Children Reserves:** All units in the enemy player's army have the Outflank special rule.

**Lines of Retreat:** Any Clan Raukaan units that fall back must do so towards the centre of the board. Any enemy units that fall back must do so towards the nearest short table edge.

**Outnumbered & Outgunned:** Each time an enemy troops, elites or fast attack unit is completely destroyed, remove it from play and place it into Ongoing Reserves, where it will be available to return to the battle at the start of enemy player's next turn.

**No Retreat, No Surrender:** Every non-vehicle unit in the Clan Raukaan army has the Zealot special rule.

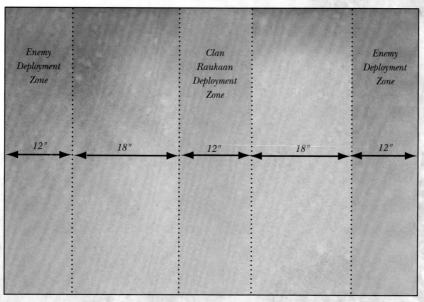

# ECHOES OF WAR:
# THE HAMMER FALLS

The enigmatic Eldar of Craftworld Alaitoc have assailed the garden world of Dawnbreak, seemingly without cause. Despite the Imperium sending swift reinforcements in the guise of the Catachan 17th Army Group, even the elite jungle fighters prove to be no match for the evasive hit and run tactics employed by the Eldar. The Catachans are soon forced to call for aid, and are answered by a powerful battle group of Clan Raukaan. To the planet's embattled defenders, deliverance seems to be at hand…

Yet rather than lend support to the Imperial Guard ground forces as expected, the warriors of Clan Raukaan ignore them completely, launching an immediate full-strength attack on an unassuming excavation site instead. Quite why the Eldar are so protective of this dig site is uncertain, but the Iron Hands seem to know a lot more about what lies buried there than the planet's oblivious population.

*Designer's Note: You will need a copy of the Planetstrike rules to play this scenario.*

## THE ARMIES

Choose armies as described in the Fighting a Battle section of the *Warhammer 40,000* rulebook, but following the army selection specifications detailed in the Planetstrike rules. The Clan Raukaan player is the Attacker, and must choose a primary detachment from *Codex: Space Marines* using the extra rules presented in this book. The enemy player is the Defender, and must choose a primary detachment from *Codex: Eldar*. In addition, the enemy player must include a Farseer as his Warlord.

## THE BATTLEFIELD

Use the deployment map included in this mission. Set up terrain as described in the Fighting a Battle section of the *Warhammer 40,000* rulebook.

### PLACE PRIMARY OBJECTIVE

After setting up the terrain, the enemy player must place a single objective marker in the centre of the battlefield to represent the dig site.

## DEPLOYMENT

Before any models are deployed, both players roll to determine Warlord Traits and select their Planetstrike Stratagems. Each player has 4 Stratagem Points.

The Attacker selects any one table edge to be his. The Defender's table edge is the one opposite the Attacker's.

The enemy player then deploys in the manner described in the Planetstrike rules. The Clan Raukaan player's army begins the game in Reserve.

## FIRST TURN

The Clan Raukaan player, as Attacker, has the first turn.

## GAME LENGTH

This mission uses Variable Game Length as described in the *Warhammer 40,000* rulebook.

## VICTORY CONDITIONS

At the end of the game, the player who has scored the most Victory Points wins the game. If players have the same number of Victory Points, the game is a draw.

### PRIMARY OBJECTIVES
**At the end of the game, the player who controls the objective marker receives 3 Victory Points.**

### SECONDARY OBJECTIVES
**Slay the Warlord, First Blood.**

## MISSION SPECIAL RULES

**Night Fighting, Reserves, Mysterious Objectives.**

**Planetstrike:** The mission uses the following special rules from the Planetstrike rules: **Firestorm, Planetary Assault, Shock Assault, Scramble.**

*Defender's Table Edge*

Objective

*Clan Raukaan Table Edge*

# RUTHLESS LOGIC

The forge world of Columnus lies in the path of an Ork armada of titanic proportions. Clan Company Raukaan moves to support their brothers of the Adeptus Mechanicus without delay, though it is only when they reach the planet's surface that they realise they are not alone in this venture. Space Marines of the Raven Guard Chapter have been battling to slow the progress of the Ork Waaagh! for many weeks, and are preparing themselves to make a stand and defend the vital forge world against the impending greenskin invasion.

Soon after the so-called Weirdwaaagh! makes its destructive planetfall, the greenskin leader – a powerful Warphead by the name of Zagdakka – spearheads an assault against the fortress factory of Urdri and blasts an enormous breach with a coruscating beam of Waaagh! energy. The Raven Guard react without hesitation to plug the gaping hole in Urdri's defences, but Iron Father Kristos has other ideas, callously leaving his brother Space Marines to die whilst he readies the warriors of Clan Raukaan for the perfect moment to strike.

## ARMIES

Choose armies as described in the Fighting a Battle section of the *Warhammer 40,000* rulebook. The Clan Raukaan player must choose a primary detachment from *Codex: Space Marines* using the extra rules presented in this book. This detachment must include a Master of the Forge with the Tempered Helm (see page 50) as the Warlord, to represent Iron Father Kristos. The Clan Raukaan player cannot include an allied detachment. The enemy player must choose a primary detachment from *Codex: Orks*, and must include a Weirdboy as his Warlord to represent Zagdakka.

Finally, the Clan Raukaan player must choose a separate 500-point detachment of Raven Guard from *Codex: Space Marines*. This detachment must include a Space Marine Captain with jump pack as its Warlord, to represent Shadow Captain Stenn, but cannot include any Drop Pods, Flyers or fortifications.

## THE BATTLEFIELD

Use the deployment map included in this mission. Set up terrain as described in the Fighting a Battle section of the *Warhammer 40,000* rulebook.

### PLACE PRIMARY OBJECTIVES

After setting up the terrain, the Clan Raukaan player must place three objective markers anywhere within his 12" of his table edge, but at least 12" apart.

## DEPLOYMENT

Before any models are deployed, both players roll to determine Warlord Traits. Note that the Clan Raukaan player has two separate forces, each with its own Warlord (Shadow Captain Stenn and Iron Father Kristos) and must roll to determine a Warlord Trait for each one.

The Clan Raukaan player deploys all of his Raven Guard units (no units can be held in Reserve), using the rules from the *Warhammer 40,000* rulebook and the deployment map opposite. Neither the Orks nor the Iron Hands are deployed at this stage – both forces are in Reserve and move on during the course of the game (see the Mission Special Rules below).

## FIRST TURN

The enemy player has the first turn.

## GAME LENGTH

This mission uses Variable Game Length as described in the *Warhammer 40,000* rulebook. However, do not count any turns until the last Raven Guard model has been removed as a casualty – the following (Clan Raukaan) player turn counts as the start of Turn 1 for the purposes of Variable Game Length.

## VICTORY CONDITIONS

At the end of the game, the player who has scored the most Victory Points wins the game. If players have the same number of Victory Points, the game is a draw.

### PRIMARY OBJECTIVES

At the end of the game, each objective marker is worth 3 Victory Points to the player that controls it.

### SECONDARY OBJECTIVES
**Slay the Warlord\*, First Blood, Linebreaker.**

\* In this mission, the Slay the Warlord Secondary Objective is worth 3 Victory Points to the Clan Raukaan player. The enemy player earns 1 Victory Point for killing the Raven Guard Warlord, or 3 Victory Points for killing both of the Clan Raukaan player's Warlords.

# MISSION SPECIAL RULES

**Mysterious Objectives, Night Fighting, Reserves.**

**Into the Breach:** Instead of making Reserve Rolls from the start of his Turn Two, the enemy player makes Reserve Rolls from the start of his Turn One. If, by the time the enemy player rolls to see if the last of his units in Reserve arrive each turn, none of his units have done so that turn, do not make a Reserve Roll – that unit arrives automatically. The enemy player's units enter play from any point along the Wall Breach section of his table edge, as depicted on the deployment map.

**Waaagh! Zagdakka:** Each time a unit of Ork Boyz is completely destroyed (Dedicated Transports are ignored), remove it from play and place it into Ongoing Reserves, where it will be available to return to the battle at the start of the enemy player's next turn. These units enter play from any point along the Wall Breach section of the enemy player's table edge, as depicted on the deployment map.

**Mega-Warphead:** Zagdakka is a Psyker (Mastery Level 3), and can re-roll failed Psychic tests.

**Last Stand:** All non-vehicle Raven Guard units have the Fearless special rule.

**Target Optimisation… 100%:** The turn after the last Raven Guard unit is destroyed, the Clan Raukaan army arrives from Reserve. Do not roll to see if each unit is available – the entire Clan Raukaan army arrives automatically (including any Flyers or Super-heavy Flyers). The Clan Raukaan player's units enter play from any point along his table edge, as depicted on the deployment map.

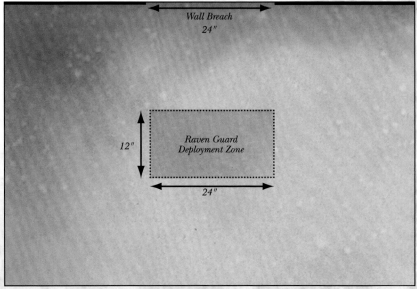

*Enemy Table Edge*

*Wall Breach*
*24"*

*12"*

*Raven Guard Deployment Zone*

*24"*

*Clan Raukaan Table Edge*

## ECHOES OF WAR:
# AN ANCIENT EVIL REVEALED

Upon hearing rumours of the accursed Sapphire King's presence, the Iron Hands translate to the Gaudinia System without delay and in great force. In this Emperor-forsaken realm, the Iron Hands seek to do battle with the faceless menace that has plagued their Chapter through the millennia, yet ever remained in the shadows. It is on Gaudinia Prime that Clan Company Raukaan discovers the terrible fate of the planet's missing populace. Bound and melded to diabolical amalgams of machine and daemonic flesh, countless billions of innocent lives have been sacrificed in order for the Sapphire King to lure the Iron Hands into its deadly trap. When it is sprung, the effects are both instantaneous and grievous for the sons of Ferrus Manus.

Through a baleful curse, many of the Chapter's Iron Fathers – Kristos himself among them – are corrupted, their seemingly infallible logic and reason turned against them, causing them to mutate into mewling machine-spawn. Only the swift thinking of Kardan Stronos steels his surviving battle-brothers against the danger and, using controlled fury as their weapon against the Daemon's influence, the Iron Hands fight their way clear. Outside the vast manufactorum, the Iron Hands regroup, Clan Company Raukaan at the fore, and prepare to take the fight to the Sapphire King and thwart its dire machinations.

## THE ARMIES

Choose armies as described in the Fighting a Battle section of the *Warhammer 40,000* rulebook. The Clan Raukaan player must choose a primary detachment from *Codex: Space Marines* using the extra rules presented in this book. This detachment must include a Chapter Master with the Axe of Medusa (see page 50) as the Warlord to represent Kardan Stronos, and a Librarian with the Mindforge Stave (see page 50) to represent Epistolary Lydriik.

The enemy player must choose a primary detachment from *Codex: Chaos Daemons*. The enemy player must include a Keeper of Secrets as the Warlord to represent the Sapphire King, and at least two other units with the Daemon of Slaanesh special rule. The enemy player can choose to include an allied detachment comprising units with the Mark of Slaanesh special rule chosen from *Codex: Chaos Space Marines*.

## THE BATTLEFIELD

Use the deployment map included in this mission. Set up terrain as described in the Fighting a Battle section of the *Warhammer 40,000* rulebook.

## DEPLOYMENT

Before any models are deployed, the Clan Raukaan player should roll to determine his Warlord Trait. The enemy Warlord automatically has the Immortal Commander Warlord Trait (see *Codex: Chaos Daemons*).

Both players then deploy their forces as described in the Fighting a Battle section of the *Warhammer 40,000* rulebook.

## FIRST TURN

The player that deployed first has the first turn unless their opponent can Seize the Initiative as described in the *Warhammer 40,000* rulebook.

## GAME LENGTH

This mission uses Variable Game Length as described in the *Warhammer 40,000* rulebook.

## VICTORY CONDITIONS

At the end of the game, the player who has scored the most Victory Points wins the game. If players have the same number of Victory Points, the game is a draw.

### PRIMARY OBJECTIVE

**At the end of the game, each player receives 1 Victory Point for each enemy unit that has been completely destroyed.** Units that are falling back at the end of the game, and units that are not on the board at the end of the game, count as destroyed for the purposes of this mission. Remember that Independent Characters and Dedicated Transports are individual units and award Victory Points if they are destroyed.

### SECONDARY OBJECTIVES
Slay the Warlord*, First Blood, Linebreaker.

\* In this mission the Slay the Warlord Secondary Objective is worth 3 Victory Points to the Clan Raukaan player.

## MISSION SPECIAL RULES
**Reserves.**

**The Sapphire King:** At the start of each of the enemy player's turns, every non-vehicle Clan Raukaan unit within 12" of the enemy Warlord (including Independent Characters that have joined squads), must pass a Leadership test. If the test is failed, the affected unit suffers 1 Wound with no saves allowed. These Wounds are Randomly Allocated. Furthermore, if this causes an Independent Character, or the last model in a unit, to be removed as a casualty, then that model is turned into a Chaos Spawn under the enemy player's control (see below). If the Leadership test is passed, the affected unit has the Zealot special rule until the start of the enemy player's next turn.

If a Clan Raukaan model is turned into a Chaos Spawn, before the model is removed, the enemy player places a new Chaos Spawn with the Mark of Slaanesh special rule (see *Codex: Chaos Space Marines*) anywhere within 6" of the slain model that is more than 1" from any unit (friendly or enemy) and more than 1" away from impassable terrain. The Chaos Spawn cannot declare a charge on the turn it arrives, but can otherwise act normally under the enemy player's control. If you do not have a spare Chaos Spawn model, the slain model does not turn into a Chaos Spawn, but is removed as a casualty as normal. The Clan Raukaan player receives 1 Victory Point for destroying each Chaos Spawn that is created in this manner. If no Chaos Spawn is created as a result of there being no spare Chaos Spawn model, no Victory Points are awarded.

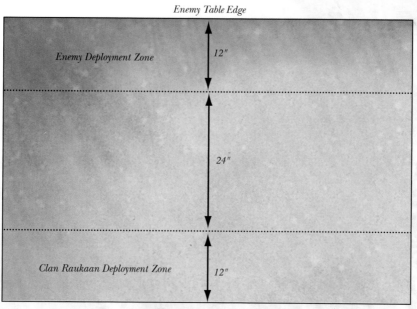

*Enemy Table Edge*

*Enemy Deployment Zone*     12"

24"

*Clan Raukaan Deployment Zone*     12"

*Clan Raukaan Table Edge*

# ECHOES OF WAR:
# IRON AND STEEL

A deathless menace has arisen on the world of Bromoch. With ancient, arcane technology, the race that the Imperium would later come to know as the Necrons has torn the very fabric of the planet asunder, Bromoch's oceans draining away in a matter of days into a vast chasm. Deep in the heart of this oceanic trench, a long-buried tomb complex reawakens, disgorging untold thousands of relentless metallic warriors onto the planet's surface to annihilate its hapless population.

Shortly after their arrival, the Iron Hands are soon plunging into the depths of the chasm, intent on delivering the Omnissiah's wrath to the heart of the xenos tomb complex. Led by Kardon Stronos, Clan Company Raukaan is tasked with holding off the legion of machines that advance upon the intruders. If the Iron Hands can hold their position long enough for the mysterious device they brought with them to be activated, then the deaths of so many of the planet's inhabitants may yet be avenged…

## THE ARMIES

Choose armies as described in the Fighting a Battle section of the *Warhammer 40,000* rulebook. The Clan Raukaan player must choose a primary detachment from *Codex: Space Marines* using the extra rules presented in this book. The Clan Raukaan player must include a Chapter Master with the Axe of Medusa (see page 50) as his Warlord to represent Kardan Stronos, but cannot include any Fortifications. The enemy player must choose a primary detachment from *Codex: Necrons*.

## THE BATTLEFIELD

Use the deployment map included in this mission. Set up terrain as described in the Fighting a Battle section of the *Warhammer 40,000* rulebook.

### PLACE PRIMARY OBJECTIVE

Place a single objective marker in the centre of the battlefield, as depicted on the deployment map.

## DEPLOYMENT

Before any models are deployed, both players should roll to determine their Warlord Traits.

The Clan Raukaan player must place all of his non-Flyer or Super-heavy Flyer units within 12" of the centre of the battlefield. The enemy player does not deploy – all of his units begin the game in Reserve.

## FIRST TURN

The enemy player has the first turn.

## GAME LENGTH

This mission uses Variable Game Length as described in the *Warhammer 40,000* rulebook.

## VICTORY CONDITIONS

At the end of the game, the player who has scored the most Victory Points wins the game. If players have the same number of Victory Points, the game is a draw.

### PRIMARY OBJECTIVES

At the end of the game, the objective marker is worth 3 Victory Points to the player that controls it.

### SECONDARY OBJECTIVES

Slay the Warlord, First Blood.

## MISSION SPECIAL RULES

Night Fighting, Reserves.

**Anti-Intruder Protocols:** Instead of making Reserve Rolls from the start of his Turn Two, the enemy player makes Reserve Rolls from the start of his Turn One. If, by the time the enemy player rolls to see if the last of his units in Reserve arrive each turn, none of his units have done so that turn, do not make a Reserve Roll – that unit arrives automatically. The enemy player's units enter play from any point along any table edge.

**Clan Raukaan Reserves:** The Clan Raukaan player must bring on units held in Reserve/Ongoing Reserves from any point along the southern table edge (see map).

**Lines of Retreat:** Any Clan Raukaan units that Fall Back must do so towards the centre of the board. Any enemy units that Fall Back do so towards the nearest table edge.

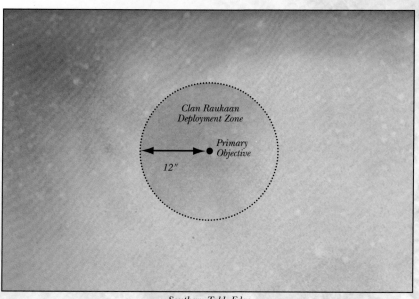

*Clan Raukaan
Deployment Zone*

*Primary
Objective*

*12"*

*Southern Table Edge*